TUNISIA

I   (frontispiece, overleaf) 'Ghorfas' in Medenine

Nina Nelson

TUNISIA

B. T. Batsford Ltd
London

TO KEITH AND PAM DOUGLAS

First published 1974
© Nina Nelson 1974

Made and printed in Great Britain by
Cox and Wyman Ltd, London, Fakenham and Reading
for the publishers B. T. Batsford Ltd
4 Fitzhardinge Street, London W.1

ISBN 0 7134 2812 0

Contents

The Plates

The Maps

Acknowledgements

While writing this book I have had unstinted help from many people – not least from Tunisians I met cursorily on my travels. I owe special thanks to Jeffrey Rayner, who looks after Tunisian tourism public relations in the United Kingdom and, with his customary enthusiasm, made plans to enable me to see as much of the country as possible. To the Tunisian tourist authorities who smoothed my path in so many directions. In particular I would like to thank Mr Azzabi the Director and Mr Goubaa who, despite my changing plans, remained unruffled and Mr Slouma who also brought a magic wand to bear. My thanks to Tijani Haddad and, in London, to the director of the Tunisian National Tourist Office, R. Ben Salah, who was always more than helpful, as was his assistant Jennifer Woolgar. K. Benattia who patiently found answers to my questions and to James Holloway whose additional information on various places mentioned has been more than useful. I am grateful to His Excellency Archibald Mackenzie, recently British Ambassador to Tunisia, who had such interesting tales to tell, and also to Betty Low for her help with research. Marie Chitty, hard pressed with teaching duties, still found time to decipher my many notes and type the manuscript. My thanks to Stuart Hulse who launched Tunis Air's new U.K. direct service and their manager in London, Amor Azak. Last but certainly not least I am grateful to Monique Cubitt for information on wild boar hunting in Tabarka.

The author and publishers are grateful to the following for supplying photographs reproduced in the book: Anne Bolt for plates 4, 7 and 8; Douglas Dickins for plates 1, 11, 12, 16, 18, 19 and 20; James Holloway for plates 23 and 24; and A. F. Kersting for plates 2, 9, 13–15, 17, 21 and 22. Plates 3, 5, 6 and 10 are from photographs taken by the author. The maps were drawn by Patrick Leeson.

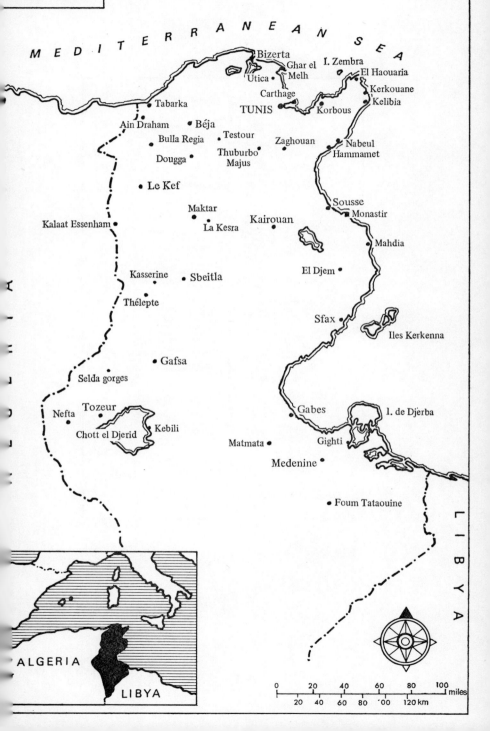

TUNISIA

MEDITERRANEAN SEA

Bizerta
Ghar el Melh
I. Zembra
El Haouaria
Utica
Carthage
Kerkouane
Kelibia
TUNIS
Korbous
Tabarka
Ain Draham
Béja
Zaghouan
Nabeul
Bulla Regia
Testour
Hammamet
Dougga
Thuburbo Majus
Le Kef
Maktar
Kairouan
Sousse
Monastir
Kalaat Essenham
La Kesra
Mahdia
Kasserine
Sbeitla
El Djem
Thélepte
Sfax
Iles Kerkenna
Gafsa
Selda gorges
Nefta
Tozeur
Gabes
I. de Djerba
Chott el Djerid
Kebili
Matmata
Gighti
Medenine
Foum Tataouine
LIBYA
ALGERIA
LIBYA

0 20 40 60 80 100 miles
20 40 60 80 100 120 km

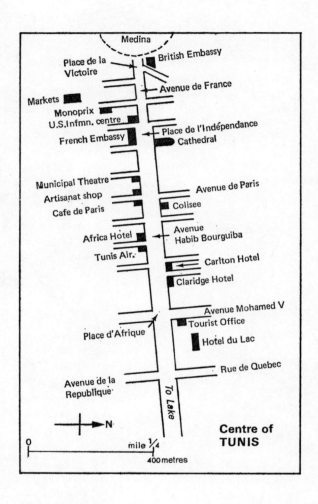

Medina

Place de la Victoire

British Embassy

Avenue de France

Markets

Monoprix

U.S. Infmn. centre

French Embassy

Place de l'Indépendance

Cathedral

Municipal Theatre

Artisanat shop

Cafe de Paris

Avenue de Paris

Colisee

Africa Hotel

Tunis Air.

Avenue Habib Bourguiba

Carlton Hotel

Claridge Hotel

Avenue Mohamed V

Tourist Office

Place d'Afrique

Hotel du Lac

Rue de Quebec

Avenue de la Republique

To Lake

N

Centre of TUNIS

0   mile ¼

400 metres

1. History and Culture

Tunisia, covering an area of 51,000 square miles, is edged by the Mediterranean in the north, by Algeria to the west, Libya in the east and by the Sahara in the south. Its average length is roughly 400 miles and its breadth 150. On maps Tunisia is drawn in a lozenge shape. Indeed President Bourguiba once described his country as 'that tiny stamp, stuck on to the top edge of the continent of Africa'. The description is apt. Although small, a stamp is a very important part of any envelope for without it the letter cannot reach its destination. Tunisia has always played a leading role in Arab and African affairs. Even the word 'Africa' goes back to Carthaginian days and is derived from the Roman corruption of the old Berber word 'Ifriqa'.

Visitors to the country find such magnificent Roman remains as those at El Djem, Sbeitla and Dougga unforgettable. For the adventurous traveller there are the attractive oases and Berber villages and for those who are interested in folklore there are as many colourful customs as could be found anywhere. The blasé will find trendy discotheques and night clubs, the gourmet several unusual dishes. There are lively shopping souks and excursions, not only for sightseeing but for those interested in fishing trips or a wild boar hunt. Yet perhaps to the tourist of today Tunisia's greatest attraction lies in its smooth sandy beaches – over 700 miles in length and therefore uncluttered. Few visitors can resist that fascinating place in the south, the Odyssey's island of the lotus eaters – Jerba. Here again the allure is not only palm-fringed open spaces but the unpolluted sandy shore seemingly stretching on for ever. Tunisia's beaches offer safe swimming in sunny, warm weather and the country's geographical position gives it a longer season than Spain or other Mediterranean rivieras – virtually from March to October. There is no overcrowding and hotels are not obtrusive for the very good reason that there is a strict ruling on the positioning of buildings and their height. At Hammamet, the most popular resort, hotels may not protrude above the tops of the palm trees.

Tunisia may be comparatively new in the tourist field but its history goes back thousands of years. It is known that men lived there in the early Paleolithic era. Flint tools like those found in Europe have been unearthed in the Gafsa region and dolmens survive from prehistoric times. In ancient days the country was known as Numidia. Later Numidians were called 'Berbers', a derivation from the Roman word 'barbari' – meaning someone not belonging to Roman civilization.

The Numidians were divided into tribes each with a reigning prince. Little of their background remains but it is known that they lived inland and were great horsemen. They successfully resisted invaders by retiring to easily defended mountainous regions. These wandering inhabitants were at first subject to the Carthaginians, but from 201 to 46 B.C. were under a native monarchy, in alliance with Rome.

From earliest times Tunisia has been coveted because of its strategic position controlling the Sicilian narrows. The sparsely populated coastal areas were rightly regarded as great prizes by the early Phoenician explorers from Syria. Phoenician colonies were founded in Tunisia 1,000 years before Christ. Famed Carthage became the most important settlement outside the Levant and as the 'granary of Rome' north Africa had no equal. According to Pliny (who is also often quoted as saying 'There is always something new from Africa') one grain of African wheat could produce a stalk bearing 150! Tunisia supplied Rome with most of its olive oil as well as fruit, wine and wood. In return Rome built cities, roads and great cisterns. Part of Tunis' water supply is still fed to the city via underground portions of a Roman aqueduct.

Three centuries before Carthage Phoenician explorers founded Utica, north of modern Tunis. The Phoenicians were among the early sailor adventurers probably because most of their towns, such as Tyre and Sidon, were along their coastline. These they found convenient for trading and reasonably easy to defend. They occupied many prominent sites in the Mediterranean and along the coast of Sicily where they had no competitors.

Legend has it that Pygmalion, a king of Tyre, murdered his brother-in-law, a priest of Melkarth, to confiscate his wealth. Pygmalion's sister Elissa, later known as Queen Dido, discovered the plot, seized her late husband's treasure and, as so many Phoenicians in the past, fled to sea accompanied by several royal companions. They spent a short time in Cyprus and then went on to Utica. They eventually founded a city close by, which was to become the famous Carthage.

Carthage was to rise to power quickly by reason of her unique position. The Phoenicians chose a promontory of red rock in the Bay of Tunis where Africa reaches out towards Sicily. To the north were impassable sea marshes, while to the south the large lagoon of Tunis formed a splendid natural harbour. Landward an isthmus, only three miles wide, could be defended easily. By the almost land-locked lake harbour the newcomers built on a low hill and from the start established friendly and commercial relations with the Berber horsemen of Numidia.

The new city became rich, magnificent palaces and temples arose. The central low-walled hill called Borsa, the fort, grew into a mighty citadel. Down from the citadel, with its arched recesses and parapets, to the marketplace ran three streets edged with mansions six storeys high, each impregnable for they overhung steep ravines. Beyond the marketplace slaves excavated a great waterway 1,066 feet wide in a cuplike shape which encircled an island. It was called the Cothon, or drinking cup. From a palace-fortress on the island the leader of the Carthaginian fleet could study the shipping *en route* to the city. In the harbour were three- and five-tiered rowing galleys with metal beaks for ramming an oncoming enemy. Fronting each dock there were ionic columns supporting a circular colonnade that connected with a strong outer wall which hid what was going on within from prying eyes. High-ranking officers could control the work by the aid of trumpets. The sea entrance could be closed quickly by chains as it was a bare 70 feet wide.

Carthage gradually ousted Tyre in the western Mediterranean, yet relations remained friendly and Carthage sent tributes to the mother country for the temple of Melkarth. When Cambyses marched into Egypt he tried to persuade the Phoenicians, who were the major portion of his fleet, to attack Carthage but they refused. Later when Tyre, besieged by Alexander, was in grave danger Tyrians sent their womenfolk, children and old men to Carthage for safety.

Religious beliefs in Carthage were the same as in Tyre and were connected with the power and processes of nature. Gods and goddesses were believed to exist in such places as mountains and rivers. Melkarth combined celestial with marine qualities. The abominable rites of sacrificing first-born children by fire and branding to the moon goddess Tanit was practised in times of stress. Despite this horrible custom Tanit had noble aspects such as being the goddess of wedded love. She was depicted as a woman archangel with crimson, blue and gold wings enfolded about her body.

Carthaginians of the nobility had magnificent estates beyond the city worked by slaves. Judges were drawn from this hierarchy and were elected in pairs. Twenty senators were also chosen but the real governing body was an assembly of 104 leading merchants known as 'The Hundred'. Aristotle mentions the Carthaginians being 'a well-governed people'. The harbours were not only full of trading ships but also of vessels used to found colonies overseas. In the fifth century two expeditions were recorded, one of which sailed to the west coast of Europe and the other, led by an adventurer called Hanno, down the African coast. Hanno passed the Senegal River and probably reached the Cameroons. He described a volcano and also a gorilla – a creature not known before.

2   *Interior of the Great Mosque in Tunis*

Life ceased to be idyllic for the Carthaginians when they had their first conflict with the Greeks in Sicily and were utterly routed before returning home. Later came the three Punic wars. Prior to the first one the Carthaginians had never been beaten at sea. They were skilled sailors and in seamanship remained unequalled until the coming of the Vikings. Rome had come into being a century after Carthage and, infuriated by the Carthaginians' sudden destructive raids not only on Sicily but on the Italian coastline itself, decided to attack them at sea. The Romans were well aware of the skill of the Carthaginians in ramming tactics and swift manoeuvring on the water but they had a trick up their sleeve which gave them unquestionable superiority. Each Roman ship was equipped with a boarding bridge which could be swung around and, by means of a sharp claw, grapple with an enemy ship. During the battle as soon as two opponent ships faced each other the Roman bridge was dropped and fully armed Romans rushed across it overpowering the thinly clad, surprised Carthaginians.

Rome, encouraged by this naval victory at Mylae, despatched Regulus, a well-known general, with several legions to land on the coast of Africa and begin operations against Carthage, in earnest. Fortune favoured the Romans for a time but their conditions for surrender were so severe that the Carthaginians resolved to fight on. The Romans were forced to retreat but were determined to keep Sicily. The Carthaginians were equally determined that they should not and invaded the island. The First Punic War dragged on with reverses and victories on both sides for the next 16 years. As Carthage fought with the aid of mercenaries most of her damage was on the financial side. The Romans suffered heavy losses at sea. Carthage eventually produced an outstandingly adroit general, Hamilcar, who resolved to bring the Romans to their knees. At first things went well. New mercenaries, most of whom belonged to the desert tribes close to Carthage, were inspired by Hamilcar. But Rome also made a great effort to have supremacy. Their treasury was empty but private citizens loosened their purse strings and enabled a fleet of 200 ships to sail to the attack. Once again the

3   Bird cage factory in Tunis

Carthaginians were taken by surprise and 24 years of fighting ensued at the end of which they agreed to pay an enormous war indemnity to Rome and to surrender Sicily which they had occupied on and off for 400 years.

Hamilcar knew that peace could only be temporary. One day the Romans would again attempt a conquest of Africa and the downfall of Carthage. It became necessary to strengthen his hand and, as Rome had a footing firmly in the Mediterranean, he thought it wise to look further afield. Spain might be the answer.

Hamilcar crossed the Straits of Gibraltar and for nine long years sought to establish a large province in Spain. Not only did he manage to support his army by the spoils but also sent money back to Carthage. Before he realized his dream he was killed in a skirmish and his son-in-law, Hasdrubal, carried on the grandiose enterprise. After warring for a further eight years the subjugation of Spain was more or less complete. Although Rome was highly suspicious of the Carthaginian exploits in Spain they were mollified when told it was the only way Carthage could pay her war indemnity. Rome took the precaution, however, of warning Hasdrubal not to push his conquests further than the River Ebro.

Hasdrubal was assassinated and Hannibal, the eldest son of Hamilcar, was acclaimed commander-in-chief by the soldiers. His appointment was confirmed by the Carthaginian government.

Hannibal, who had commanded the cavalry under Hasdrubal, was 29 years old and was to become one of the world's greatest generals. He inherited a highly trained army and the men were devoted to him. He spent his first two years as commander-in-chief completing the conquest of Spain south of the Ebro. He then set himself to what he felt to be his life's duty – to fight and humiliate the Romans.

Hannibal started by besieging Saguntum, a city allied to Rome. Saguntum held out for eight months and Rome sent envoys to Carthage demanding an explanation. There was no satisfactory answer and so the Second Punic War began and lasted from 219 to 201 B.C.

Hannibal did not expose himself to the perils of the sea as so

4   A ceiling in the Bardo Palace, Tunis

many had before him but determined to reach Italy through the Alps. He negotiated with several Celtic tribes for assistance or neutrality since he had to cross the Ebro and the Pyrenees, not to mention southern France, before he began his ascent of the Alps. The first part of his plan miscarried, for many of the so-called friendly or neutral tribes harried and attacked him and, before even reaching the Pyrenees, his army had shrunk by one-fourth. He then wisely permitted the sick and faint hearted to go home and entered France with 60,000 men.

In the meantime the Romans were not idle. As Hamilcar had foreseen, Rome still dreamt of Africa and had begun to prepare for an invasion. Scipio Africanus, a Roman general, began a softening-up process starting in Europe. He led his men to Marseilles to invade Spain. When Scipio got to Marseilles he learned that Hannibal had crossed the Pyrenees and was close by. He decided to contest the crossing of the Rhone and made pacts with the Celts to watch for Hannibal. But Hannibal reached the river four days' march above the point where the Romans had set their trap. Outwitting the Celts on guard Hannibal crossed the Rhone without loss.

What schoolboy has not heard of Hannibal crossing the Alps with his army and elephants? What an amazing picture these great creatures must have made plodding over the passes dragging war equipment. The Carthaginians had always relied on elephants to assist with their armies. In the vast citadel in their capital with space for 20,000 infantrymen and 4,000 cavalry there was also special stabling with fodder stores for 300 elephants. Two things plagued Hannibal even before he began crossing the Alps. Winter had set in and his men, used to the warmth of Spain and the constant sunshine of Africa, were always cold. The mountain tribes refused to consider his friendship and he had to fight much of his way through the mountains. Apart from such drawbacks, getting an army with its horses, baggage and elephants over mountains was a nightmare with all kinds of difficulties to be overcome. It is believed that Hannibal probably led his forces over the St Bernard pass – an extraordinary feat. Only half of his army got through to

5 *Guards at the Bardo Palace*

the plains of Hither Gaul and there Hannibal gave his hard-pressed men a much-needed rest.

With the coming of spring Hannibal's war hardened troops were refreshed and campaigning began again. Moving down the Po valley Hannibal forced the Romans to evacuate the plain of Lombardy. By December of the same year he was fighting the Romans on the River Trebia. He sent part of his light cavalry across the river to skirmish with the enemy and try and tempt them to pursue. This they did and suddenly found themselves in a position from which there was no escape unless reinforcements arrived quickly. The Romans, wet and cold, were no match for the high spirited Carthaginians and were routed – as were the reinforcements when they arrived. News of this victory percolated through the Celtic tribes who were weary of Roman rule and taxes and 60,000 of them joined Hannibal's army.

The following spring Hannibal decided to attack again. The two roads leading southward were blocked by the Romans but Hannibal led his troops through the marshes of the Arno. The way was as difficult as going over the Alps and disease was rife. Many sickened and died. Hannibal himself was stricken with ophthalmia and lost an eye. Reaching the heights overlooking Lake Trasimene, Hannibal awaited the arrival of his enemies. They were not long in coming and within a couple of days, just after dawn, the Romans marched into the river valley through a morning mist. When the sun rose they found they were surrounded by Hannibal's forces. Fighting was fierce and the Romans soon last heart. Many of them were drowned, others slaughtered. Victory was once more in Hannibal's grasp. There was nothing to prevent him marching on Rome. Yet he did not attack the capital. The reason is debatable. Neither Hamilcar nor Hannibal had contemplated the annihilation of Rome. Their ambition was to humble her and thwart her ambitions in Africa.

Hannibal returned to Carthage a hero and so enriched the city of his birth that the indemnity paid to Rome seemed as nothing. But like all famous men Hannibal had jealous enemies and behind his back high-ranking citizens complained to Rome that he was making plans to attack Italy again. Rome demanded his surrender and he fled to Tyre and became a member of King Antiochus's court. When the Romans attacked Syria Hannibal escaped to Bithynia but even there Roman vengeance sought him out. Rather than be taken prisoner he poisoned himself. So died the greatest military genius of the ancient world at the age of 64. Strange to relate in the same year Scipio Africanus, his most famous adversary whom he admired, also died.

The Third Punic War – 149 to 146 B.C. – came about because Carthage was not permitted by her treaty with Rome to make war without Roman consent. No one knew this better than Massinissa, a Numidian prince who ruled most of Tunisia, and he did not hesitate when he considered the stars were right to harass the Carthaginians and make inroads into their territory. Rome ignored pleas for redress and decided to take advantage of the situation by making another landing herself. The Roman Senate made speeches against Carthage, and Cato, a leading senator, used a phrase which echoed through the Senate corridors for months, 'Carthage must be destroyed'.

Massinissa's encirclement of the city became so dangerous that the citizens broke their treaty with Rome and retaliated. This gave Rome the excuse she wanted. Roman legions landed on the coast and demanded that all Carthaginian weapons of war should be handed over. The Carthaginians acquiesced and were told that in return they might build another town ten miles in from the coastline. Carthage in Cato's words 'was to be destroyed'. When this became known Carthaginian pride was cut to the quick; the people rose, killed those who had counselled submission and, closing the gates, worked 24 hours a day to forge new weapons to replace those they had given up. Buildings were torn down and their cedar beams used to build ships. Women cut off their hair to make ropes. Children were sacrificed to Tanit. Despite famine and pestilence the citizens worked on.

The siege of Carthage dragged on for three years. A young Roman general, carrying the name of the Scipio family by whom he had been adopted, finally broke the spirit of Carthage. The harbour was captured, the gates were forced and the streets stormed. Through six days of massacre and fighting the citizens held on grimly. The citadel fell. Sumptuous buildings were burnt and levelled. Finally human endeavour could go no further and Carthaginian resistance was broken. Rome was not satisfied. Scipio was commanded to destroy the city completely. It burned for 17 days and a solemn curse was put on any person who dared to rebuild it. Carthage, one of the most splendid cities of ancient times, was no more.

Triumphant Rome lost little time in setting up her headquarters in Utica, a few miles distant and originally colonized from Sidon. Punic speech gave way to Latin, and Roman colonization of Africa began around the coastal towns. They left the greater part of Tunisia to continue to be controlled by the Numidian princes. Massinissa's three grandsons had the land divided between them. The most powerful prince, Jugurtha, assassinated one and drove the other out of the country. The latter sought Rome's help and Jugurtha was forced to go to Rome and stand before the Senate. He upset his accusers by insulting them and managed to escape home. In 110 B.C. the Senate declared war against him. He was captured and brought back as a prisoner to Rome where he later died.

The ghost of Carthage, despite the cursing, razing and massacres – even the ploughing up of the ground upon which it stood – was not to rest in peace. Punic Carthage gave way to Roman Carthage which bloomed over the flattened rubble into a stately, imperial city. Its magnificence was such that it was held by Solinus to be 'the second wonder after Rome'. It was beautified with theatres, temples, baths, arches, mosaics, villas and other Roman wonders.

In ancient times every nation had an outstanding accomplishment; the Egyptians their pyramids, the Greeks their statues. The Romans built enormous arched aqueducts, some of which are still used today. It was not that the Romans preferred aqueducts to the underground conduit or that they did not realize that water rises to the level of its source for they were excellent engineers. They chose aqueducts most often because the building materials, brick, cement, concrete and mortar were both plentiful and cheap, whereas when they built underground systems, pipes were unreliable, the bronze ones expensive and cast-iron difficult to work.

The Emperor Hadrian built a long aqueduct from the inland mountains to Carthage. In 1718 Lady Mary Wortley Montagu wrote of it as

> that noble aqueduct which carried the water to Carthage over several high mountains, the length of forty miles. There are still many arches entire. We spent two hours viewing it with great attention, and Mr M. assured me that of Rome is very much inferior to it. The stones are of a prodigious size, and yet all polished, and so exactly fitted to each other, very little cement has been made use of to join them. Yet they may stand a thousand years longer, if art is not used to pull them down.

Lady Mary 'half broiled by the sun' greatly admired the view of Carthage on its isthmus and stood on the site where the castle of Borsa once was and continued in her writing – 'Strabo calls it forty miles in circuit'.

Rome continued to collaborate with the Numidians and many of them took Roman citizenship. During the six centuries that Tunisia was affiliated with Rome she gained from the flowering of Roman arts, literature and building. It was an affluent period as can be judged from the sumptuous remains at such places as Dougga and Sbeitla.

The cultural connection between Rome and North Africa remained into Christian times. There are many Christian mosaic murals in the museums. Africa had a great influence on Christian ideas. Saint Augustine was born in Tagraste, a small Numidian town, in 354 A.D. He attended the university in Carthage at the early age of 16. Later he became a lecturer and found fame in the city. He went to Rome where he founded a school. He was baptized in Milan on Easter Eve in 387; tradition associates this event with the composition of the Christian *Te Deum*. When Augustine returned to North Africa he was ordained in Hippo Regius, a town close to the borders of Tunisia and Algeria. He eventually became the bishop there and remained for the rest of his life.

Roman decadence gave way to the Vandals, a Germanic tribe who had pushed their way through Spain and invaded Africa under their King Genseric. They took Hippo Regius in 431 and Carthage in 439 and divided the Roman spoils. Eventually their rule was to stretch from Tangier to Tripoli. Although they became Christians they were Arians and persecuted orthodox believers.

In 533 the Byzantine General Belisarius landed in Africa – near present-day Mahdia – and after defeating the Vandals several times during the following year he restored the islands of Corsica and Sardinia as well as the coast of Africa to the Romans. To commemorate the occasion present-day Sousse (ancient Hadrumetum) became known as Justinianapolis, in honour of the Emperor whose army had won these victories.

For over a century Tunisia remained part of the Byzantine Empire until it was invaded by the Arabs in 647. Carthage was razed to the ground once again. Broken porticoes, temples, arches, pavilions and lovely mansions were ruthlessly plundered and parts of them reappeared in buildings along the coast and many inland towns. Plinths, marble columns and quarried masonry were used in the palaces of Pisa, Genoa and other faraway places, sometimes even emerging in European cathedrals. Carthage was never to be rebuilt.

The new inland capital, Kairouan, some 85 miles south of Tunis, was set on an open plain west of a river and luxuriant with gardens and olive groves according to Arabic writers, although it has ceased to be so lush today. The Islamic religion swept over the country, penetrating the mountainous regions and every tiny desert oasis.

At the time of the Aghlabites Kairouan became a place of pilgrimage, a sacred city referred to as the fourth holiest city in Islam. Moslems still believe that to visit this Holy City seven times is equal to going once to Mecca. Its great Mosque was founded in 670 by

Sidi Okba Ibn Nafi who, it is said, was given divine guidance to build it facing perfectly true to Mecca. The Mosque is the most sacred and one of the oldest and largest sanctuaries in Tunisia. Its central aisle is entered through a sculptured wooden door known as 'The Beautiful Gate'. By about 800 the mosque was renowned for its educational system and became the main law school of Islam – a forerunner of the famous law schools of the Great Mosques of Fez, Tunis and Al Azhar in Cairo. The sacred atmosphere of Kairouan has remained unimpaired since early times. Being built on slightly elevated land, it is not unlike Jerusalem when seen from a distance, a quiet city of domes and low embracing walls.

In 909 the Fatimites took over from the Aghlabites and made Mahdia, a coastal town, the capital in place of Kairouan. The Fatimid dynasty, followers of Mohammed's daughter of that name, were led by Obeid Allah, whose ambition was to become Caliph of all Islam.

Various Mohammedan sects succeeded one another on into the twelfth century when it was the turn of the Hafsites who paid tribute money to the king of Sicily in return for protection. King Louis ix of France, who was brother of the king of Sicily, now enters the scene. The crusades had been raging for some years and Louis was a true type of religious crusader. He had campaigned in Egypt and Syria and spent four years in the Holy Land seeking to establish the kingdom of Jerusalem, in which he had little success. In 1267 Louis, who had been led to believe that the Bey of Tunis might be converted, began the eighth and last of the Crusades by leading an expedition to Tunisia. He had barely gone ashore where Carthage had once held sway when he was struck ill with the plague and died repeating the name 'Jerusalem, Jerusalem'.

Louis' brother Charles, the king of Sicily, carried out the campaign but not as a crusader. The Bey of Tunis had ceased to pay tribute to Sicily and Charles meant to make the Bey resume this undertaking. He forced him not only to give a large indemnity for himself and the new king of France but also secured the usual annual subscription for his Sicilian exchequer.

During the fourteenth century incessant conflicts among the Berber princes weakened the country, and coastal towns were inadequately protected. Piracy in the Mediterranean flourished, based on the notorious Barbary Coast.

In the sixteenth century a family of Turkish admirals and sea rovers headed by the famous Barbarossa (Redbeard) captured the port of Tunis. He and his entourage had their headquarters on the island of Jerba in the Gulf of Gabes and with several thousand janissaries soon subdued Kairouan and other Tunisian towns. King Charles v of Spain, refusing to accept this state of affairs, recaptured Tunis, swept through the rest of the country and set up a Spanish protectorate which lasted from 1535 to 1574. In that year the Turkish Sultan decided to retake the country. His men were led by another famous pirate, Dragut, whose name also crops up constantly in Maltese history. Dragut and his corsairs were triumphant and Tunisia became part of the Ottoman Empire.

During the nineteenth century Turkish influence gradually slackened and that of France increased. After the Crimean War Turkish rights over the regency of Tunis were revived. The worried Bey sought advice from Britain and a British protectorate – prompted by the proximity of Malta – was set up under the influence of the remarkable Sir Richard Wood who was the British diplomatic agent at the court of Tunis from 1855 to 1879. The railways, gas and water works, lighthouses, industries and concessions were placed in British hands. However, at the Congress of Berlin in 1862, Britain gave France a 'free hand' in Tunisia in return for French agreement to the British lease of Cyprus.

In 1881 a French force crossed the Algerian border and advanced on Tunis, thus compelling the Bey to sign the 'Bardo Treaty' and to accept a French protectorate. The British government withdrew its consular jurisdiction in favour of the French courts and in 1885 it ceased to be represented by a diplomatic official.

Nationalism sprang to life after the First World War and in 1934 Habib Bourguiba became head of the Neo-Destour (New Constitution) party. Local politics were interrupted by the Second

World War which brought havoc to Tunisia. She fell under German control and Bizerta became a main port for the Axis forces.

In October 1942, the Allies landed in Morocco and Algeria. The battle for Tunisia began shortly after this with the Allies in the western part and the Germans in Tunis and the Eastern portion of the country. The Allies routed the Axis troops who retreated northwards. Sfax fell in April 1943, Bizerta and Tunis on 4 May. By 12 May the Germans threw in their hand and Tunisia was restored to France.

After the war Habib Bourguiba began his struggle again for the freedom of his country. His patient perseverance was rewarded on 20 March 1956 when France granted Tunisia independence. Tunisia became a republic with Habib Bourguiba as the first President. The republic is a member of the United Nations and also of the League of Arab Nations.

Habib Bourguiba was born in the little town of Monastir in 1903, the eighth child of an army officer. His father sold the family olive groves to ensure his children's education and was not to know that, in return, one of his sons would play a leading role in Arab affairs for over 30 years and become an inspiring living symbol in the development and life of Tunisia. Habib Bourguiba's avowed ambition has always been to 'get the most for the Tunisian people out of every situation', and he has stuck to this ever since he entered politics, whether in prison, in exile or as President. His sole object has been to better the lot of his countrymen. Women are no longer cloistered or veiled and are encouraged to enter such professions as medicine and teaching. They can choose any profession they wish on equal footing with men. Certainly there seem to be more women drivers than men in the cities!

Tunisia, through her historic ties with France, looks to France as her natural spokesman in dealings with the western world, such as the European Economic Community. Tunisia and France parted company with a feeling of uncertainty which later turned to mutual respect. During a three-day state visit to Paris in June 1972 the Tunisian leader was frank in his reply to President

Pompidou's speech of welcome : 'It is proof that I have achieved my goal, that of substituting for the bonds of dependence, relations of active and healthy cooperation.'

President Bourguiba's Destourian Socialism seeks to encourage progress in education and agriculture. The latter is not easy for Tunisia lies between the tropical and temperate zones, and this tends to remove with one hand what it gives with the other. Of three olive harvests perhaps only one will be truly excellent and it is the same story with cereals. Irrigation is hampered by a feast-or-famine type of water supply. There are numerous 'oueds' or river beds all over the country. These are empty during the heat of summer and glisten with sparkling salty deposits that look fairy-like in the distance but, after violent downpours of rain in the winter months, they can suddenly turn into raging torrents of unmanageable proportions and sweep across the countryside. Devastating floods in 1969 did untold damage and again in 1973, after several days of torrential rain, whole areas, especially in the rich Mejerda valley, were covered with flood waters up to 10 feet deep. Submerged land and homes are a well-known and grim spectacle. Such disasters mean that hundreds of people are homeless and whole families drowned, stocks and crops lost. The authorities do all they can to lessen the harm to crops and industry when these freak storms occur. An undoubted snag is the damage to roads, for the 'oueds' flow with such speed that they gorge out great stretches of even the best tarmac. Under these conditions it is not perhaps surprising to come upon a stretch of bumpy, rocky track in the middle of an otherwise perfectly good flat tarmac highway.

Motoring on the main routes, which tend to be flat and gently curving, edged by hard sand and gravel shoulders, is a joy and there is signposting to international standards. Filling stations are increasingly numerous – mostly Mobil, Esso, B.P., Shell and Agip. Nevertheless it is wise to keep a full tank for the long country roads. Place names are given in French and Arabic.

Driving is on the right and, as in France, priority is given to vehicles coming from the right. Headlights must be yellow. Despite the delight of uncluttered roads after the frustrations of Europe, you must be on the alert for wandering Arabs, sheep, dogs and children – not to mention camels. Roads leading to and from many tourist centres are wide and asphalted and there are speed limits of 100 kilometres an hour on the open road and 60 kilometres an hour in built-up areas. Even the second-class roads are often well tended.

Buses are available from Tunis to all main cities and the fares are low. Public buses do not have spreadeagled figures hanging on to every available inch as in many other Mediterranean countries. True, at rush hours they are crowded but at other times the visitor will find them as convenient as any other way to go sightseeing.

There are two kinds of taxi within the towns. Renault or Citroën minis, know affectionately as 'Bebes', coloured red and white, which you can summon by telephone, pick up from a rank or occasionally hail in the street. Or the larger type which you can hail if it is going in your direction and which, as you share it with others, is cheaper. These work extremely well once you get used to them. They carry five passengers and can be hailed as they go along the road. Two people sit in front with the driver, three others get into the back. There is a constant stopping and starting and stepping over knees. The shot of adrenalin in your stomach as you step out into crowded streets enables you to clamber out quickly, slam the door and be safely on the pavement in a few seconds.

In addition, larger vehicles, often Peugeot station wagons, known as louage taxis, run between control points in the main towns. They usually carry destination boards and offer a cheap and fairly rapid method of moving about the country and you can buy one or more seats on them as you would on a bus.

A self-drive car is certainly the best way of seeing the country and to hire one is simple, since most of the big hotels have Hertz or Avis desks. The same firms have offices in Tunis and the main towns and resorts. My husband and I had a Hertz car and motored 2,000 miles, including forays into the desert and a never-to-be-forgotten hazardous mountain trip to Matmata. Our Fiat 127 never let us down but driving in the desert or mountainous regions should not be undertaken lightly. A Land-Rover is often the better answer and it is wise to check with the National Guard that desert tracks or mountain routes are passable before setting off – especially if it has rained recently.

While on the subject of transport there are 1,265 miles of railways which ply between most of the tourist resorts.

Should you bring your own car by sea there are car ferries between Marseilles and Tunis which take approximately 22 hours, and services also operate from Naples, Palermo and Genoa to Tunis weekly. D.F.D.S. Seaways, the Danish shipping line, have a weekly service throughout the year from Genoa to Tunis every Friday, returning Sunday. These have swimming pools and other amenities such as ladies' haidressing salons and children's playrooms.

The Tunisian climate is fairly predictable and very pleasant throughout the year. The broad coastline controls the extremes of temperature. From the autumn, say from November until April, beautiful sunny days can alternate with short rainy periods. There is less rain in the south. Snow is scarce and only falls in the northern hilly regions. The desert, as elsewhere, has very hot days and cold nights.

As the terms 'hot', 'warm' and 'cold' mean different things to different people it may be best to give the reader a more exact idea of the weather. On the facing page are tables showing the air and sea average monthly temperatures in degrees fahrenheit.

Tunisia is blessed with innumerable date palms. In her three main oases, Gafsa, Nefta and Tozeur alone, there are over a million. From the glorious oasis of Nefta, one of the finest in the country and also known as the religious capital of the Jerid, come the Deglat dates we enjoy so much in the west during the Christmas season. This oasis has some 400,000 date palms watered by 150 natural springs.

The wine harvest amounts to around the 49-million-gallon mark each year and much of it is exported. It is extremely good, although more heady than French or German brands. Fruit, iron

Average Monthly Temperatures in Tunisia
(based on the last 50 years)

	J	F	M	A	M	J	J	A	S	O	N	D
Tabarka	53	53	56	60	65	73	78	80	76	68	60	54
Ain Draham	44	46	59	62	69	74	75	78	78	64	54	46
Bizerta	53	54	56	59	65	74	75	78	78	69	67	55
Tunis	55	56	58	66	70	74	79	79	78	77	62	54
Sousse	56	56	64	68	72	76	79	79	78	71	63	54
Kairouan	56	57	58	63	71	77	83	87	80	79	70	60
Gafsa	54	57	60	67	73	81	87	79	71	60	62	55
Tozeur	51	54	62	70	76	85	90	85	85	72	62	52
Gabes	54	56	61	70	71	76	79	83	79	75	65	55
Djerba	57	59	63	70	72	77	80	85	79	78	67	60
Hammamet	56	58	62	70	71	76	80	85	79	78	67	60

Average Temperatures of the Sea

January	59	July	78
February	60	August	80
March	62	September	82
April	63	October	74
May	65	November	65
June	71	December	60

ore and phosphates are also exported and Tunisia is the world's second largest producer of olive oil. Cellulose is made from esparto grass, and modern factories for light industries such as furniture and textiles are appearing. Nevertheless over three-quarters of the population are still employed in agriculture, fishing and stock breeding.

Some years ago the United Nations Special Fund helped in the economic renaissance of a large area in the centre of the country by introducing a method of raising subsoil water for the rearing of sheep and cattle. Another rewarding United Nations project has been the growing for fodder of the drought-resisting thornless cactus. The selected variety came from Mexico and yields after its fifth year. This has paid off even better than expected and in different parts of the country you can drive through miles of cactus hedge resembling the prickly pear – only without the prickles!

The Tunisians are an essentially friendly people and gentle by nature. A British traveller in 1738 described them as 'the most civilized nation of Barbary . . . having always had the reputation, not in living like their neighbours in open war or perpetual disputes with the Christian princes, but of cultivating their friendships and coming readily into their alliance'.

Various Tunisian sayings and proverbs which are constantly used prove that hospitality, as always with the Arab, is second nature.

> When you receive a guest, show him consideration, veneration and respect, for he is more venerable than your own father. Be generous with him, as befits his rank and your own. Even if you had to sacrifice both your eyes for him that would still be too little.
> When you wish to gain someone's loyalty, smile in his face and place your own food between the two of you.
> If you wish to enter into a commitment bring a loaf of bread, cut it and eat it up with your partner. This meal is a real contract. The meal is sovereign and to betray the man with whom one has shared water and salt is an act that is unworthy of a free man.

Many Tunisian proverbs are similar to our own, such as 'a bird in the cage is worth more than ten on the tree'; 'the generous hand does not die of hunger'; 'you make do with sandals until you find proper shoes'; and 'it is up to man to strive and up to God to bless his efforts'.

Religion plays a great part in Tunisian life. The words 'Allah is great and Mohammed is His Prophet' are sung from countless minarets each day to remind people of God. Perhaps the greatest difference between the Christian and Mohammedan is that the former tries to bend fate to his will but the Moslem feels everything is preordained. Life has certain things in store for him. He will try and place his footsteps one way but, if they diverge even slightly, he knows it is God's will. God knows best.

Ramadan is to the Mohammedan what Lent is to the Christian but far more stringent. It begins when the new moon rises in the ninth month of the Mohammedan year and then for 28 days no true believer may smoke, eat or drink between sunrise and sunset. The dates of Ramadan are different each year as the Moslems use the lunar calendar. It is a severe strain when it happens during the hottest months in the summer and not even a sip of water should be drunk during the daytime. Children, travellers and sick people are exempt from fasting.

During Ramadan night is turned into day. Fasting has ceased, the tension of the long day is forgotten and the cafés are full of carefree people. Families gather together for a substantial meal and there is the excited chatter of children who stay up with their parents. A brisk trade in food goes on in both villages and towns.

In Tunis there is a fair in the Bab Souika Square with sword swallowers, acrobats and dancers. Music is provided by the 'mezwed', an instrument resembling and sounding like the bagpipes, and 'darbukas', which are small clay drums. Moonlight seeps down through the multicoloured lights but as it wanes the square and surrounding streets gradually empty. Tunis is scarcely at rest before the sun rises on another day of Ramadan.

A festival takes place for two or three days at the end of Ramadan and there are other religious festivals during the year, but the dates are difficult to pinpoint for the same reason as Ramadan itself. Aid Es Seghir is the celebration for the end of Ramadan; Aid El Kebir is to celebrate the memory of Abraham's sacrifice; the Mouled is the anniversary of Mohammed's birth; and Ras El Am begins the Moslem New Year.

Many non-religious festivals take place annually, one of the most joyous perhaps being that of the 'Palm Tree' which is during the date harvest in the oases. The fruit is gathered to the accompaniment of song and dance. When the work is finished traditional 'couscous' is eaten or, more often, lamb is grilled over charcoal fires. When the feasting is over there are camel races and other sports. The Orange Tree Festival is held annually at Nabeul. This continues for a whole week in May and the air is fragrant with orange blossom, the townsfolk wear their best clothes and Nabeul itself is decked in its best array.

Sousse has a carnival in late March. Sfax and Jerba have celebrations in April and in May there are dramatic performances at Dougga. There is a festival of Andalusian Music in June at Testour and in August there are special celebrations in Monastir. These are in honour of President Bourguiba's birthday and include Son et Lumière in the ancient fortress.

It is useful to try and remember the public holidays as the banks, museums and main shops are closed.

1 January	New Year's Day
18 January	Festival of the Tunisian Revolution
20 March	Independence Day
9 April	Anniversary of the Martyrs
9 May	Labour Day
1 June	National Festival
3 August	President Bourguiba's Birthday
13 August	Emancipation of Women
3 September	Commemoration of the Foundation of Freedom 1934
15 October	Evacuation Festival (when the French army left the country)

As might be expected of the inhabitants of a country situated roughly opposite the mid-point of the Mediterranean where it is narrow, the Tunisians are the product of a series of conquests and occupations. Though ethnically of Arab–Berber stock, their situation of comparative accessibility and strategic importance has ensured a considerable admixture of peoples representing an amalgam which is not repeated along the North African coast. Their most recent occupation by the French has also left its mark. Many Tunisians in positions of authority today were reared under a French-oriented system of education, and their bureaucracy,

6   *A doorway in Sidi bou Said*

administration and many other aspects of life owe much to their late mentors. Arabic is the official language but French is almost universally spoken, though a start has now been made on English – especially in the towns and resorts.

Over 90 per cent of the people are Moslems and there are about 4 million inhabitants – less than in Denmark or Switzerland – and it is reckoned that some 50 per cent are under 20 years of age. There are some 50,000 Jews, a few thousand Protestants and some 75,000 Roman Catholics. Every creed is free to worship in its own way. In Tunis for instance there is an Anglican Church, St George's, and a Roman Catholic Cathedral.

Education is eagerly sought and you can see new schools all over the country. At certain times of day streams of children clad in blue or pink 'tabliers' are going or coming from school, each child swinging a school satchel and usually wearing short plastic wellingtons which must be unbearably hot during the summer.

The village women wear what is called a 'Sifsari', a length of material, usually white, about the size of a large tablecloth, which is used to cover the whole body even if there is a modern frock underneath. It also covers the head and part of the face, a fold being held by the teeth. It is fascinating to watch the deftness in turning the head to talk and then swinging back again and picking up the corner of cloth in the teeth as if it had never dropped. Strangely enough the 'Sifsari' is not as long as such coverings in other Middle Eastern countries where they reach the ankles. Whether the mini skirt has had an effect or not the 'Sifsari' often stops just below the knee and thus the uniformity of the top half is rudely shattered by a wide variety of colourful footwear ranging from plaid carpet slippers to the latest wooden platform sandals or gold evening shoes. In various districts the 'Sifsari' can be of different colours and designs. Many women go unveiled and at the other extreme, Bizerta being one, they cover their faces completely.

European dress has been adopted by both men and women, particularly in the towns, but traditional robes are still widely worn and are far better adapted to the climate. For instance in

7   *The main street of Sidi bou Said*

cold weather not only are hooded burnouses of camel hair worn but often rectangular-shaped camel rugs are wound about the body for warmth. Centuries of use have taught the right way of using these to get complete covering and a corner is often thrown over the shoulder with great élan.

The Koran says 'Man cannot exist without constant effort', and this might well be the adage of the farm labourer. He begins his days at sunrise and works steadily on until sunset. Clad in his short-sleeved, loose cotton robe he is a familiar sight working in the fields, olive groves or among the date palms. His red 'chechia', round pillbox-like hat, adds a dash of bright colour to the landscape. The 'chechia' is not as much protection against the sun as the 'mud-hala', a flat or sometimes beehive-shaped straw hat with a wide brim, worn in many villages. In the southern part of the country you often see the 'kafiya', a square of material worn as a head covering in biblical fashion.

In the towns the ordinary wear for men not in western clothes is a type of trouser secured under the knee and over it a thin long jacket reaching just below the trouser legs, leaving the leg bare from knee to ankle. Far more attractive is the 'gondura' a long, loose silken robe, reaching to the ankles.

The Tunisian monetary unit is the Dinar (worth approximately £1 but this can fluctuate) divided into 1,000 millièmes.

Though Tunisia is close to Europe its music tends to the oriental, but a form of it, 'Malouf', is undeniably Andalusian, brought across the Mediterranean by the Moors. The 'danse du ventre' is always part of any dance celebration, whether folkloric or as part of an hotel cabaret. Equally authentic, but more unusual, are the age-old Sahara dances of the sword and the firearm, which are more likely to be seen in the southern part of the country.

Since childhood one has associated the camel with the desert, and happily his role has not changed and he continues to play a great part in the country's economy. He holds his head in such a disdainful manner, the Arab says, because, although Man may know the 99 names of Allah, the camel knows the hundredth! The weight he can carry with ease is phenomenal and his slithering cushion-footed gait enables him to plod through the city streets with as much ease as over burning sand. His hide provides leather, rugs and the 'burnous' (a camel is shorn every year). Camel dung is used for fires and as a fertilizer. The camel possesses more endurance than any other creature although when he finally flags nothing will resuscitate him — hence the old adage — 'the straw that broke the camel's back'! The Arab uses camel milk to drink and make cheese. Although the camel takes 16 or 17 years to come to full maturity, he will live until he is 50 or 60. If overtaken by a sandstorm he will fall on his knees, stretch his neck along the sand, close his nostrils and eyes and remain motionless until the storm ceases. In the meantime he provides shelter for his master who, wrapped in his burnous, lies down-wind of the beast. He has very, very long eyelashes to keep the sand out of his eyes and he uses them with allure when posing for the photographer in the brightest sunlight for, unlike other animals, he never seeks shade.

The female camel carries her young for 11 months and produces one calf which she suckles for a year. The baby camel stands about 3 feet high after a week or so. It is a fuzzy little creature and adds very much to the scene. If you are fortunate enough to drive near the camel-herding area, those fantastically lovely sunsets across the desert with strings of camels along the horizon which you see in glossy magazines, become a reality. Such herds can be over 100 strong.

Lions and leopards are a thing of the past in the mountains south of Tabarka where today the wild boar rules supreme. Goats are forbidden because of the damage they do to trees but you still see them here and there. The usual domestic animals flourish in the sunny climate. Of the reptile family there are snakes, scorpions, lizards, geckos and chameleons, but these are seldom seen by the average visitor. However it is advisable to be cautious near thickets or piles of stones.

Birds are numerous and vary in size from pelicans to the smallest water bird. Migratory birds include the quail which occasionally features on hotel menus. Sometimes, as the light begins to fade in the evening, what you imagine to be pink and white clouds turn out to be flocks of flamingoes – one of the prettiest sights in Tunisia.

Olive groves lining the highway soon become a familiar sight for the visiting motorist, their silvery-green leaves cool against the blue of the sky, however hot the day. It is said that the presence of the olive tree indicates that you are close to the Mediterranean. Unquestionably it lends this feeling of coolness to the scene, especially in the early spring when its tiny cream-coloured flowers open. Olive trees have inspired painters, poets and writers, the Spanish author Miguel de Unamuno going so far as to say that they have a personality.

The wild olive is an unproductive evergreen belonging, improbably enough, to the same family as the jasmine and forsythia. It is believed that about 3500 B.C. a Cretan discovered that a branch of a certain fruit tree could be grafted on to the wild olive, which had a miraculous effect and produced the large olive we know today. This was the beginning of the spread of olive culture around the Mediterranean and was so rewarding that the olive branch became the symbol of peace, for with the olive came prosperity and amicable relations, the foundations of peace.

Tunisia's most famous olive groves are near Sousse and Sfax. Most surprisingly they can also be seen for miles on the road to Zarzis. A new experiment was tried here in the 1950s when the French settled a number of Accara Bedouin in this district to tend new groves planted in what was always said to be unproductive sandy soil. The trees seemed to grow overnight, their long roots seeking and finding sources of subsoil water. The desert sand from which they appear to spring is scrupulously neat and tilled. No one farmer agrees with the other about the cultivation of his olive trees. One man will plough once a season, another two or three times. Some use irrigation, others not; when to harvest, early or late, is a moot point.

The mountains in the north-west are covered with oak and pine but in general the country is sparsely wooded, yet the variety of trees is astonishing : cork oaks, eucalyptus, poplars, ashes and elms. Not only the palm but the acacia, with its mimosa-like blossoms, grow among the scrub and camel-thorn in the desert. An interesting but little-known fact about the palm tree is that, when necessary, its roots will go down 50 feet or more to find water. The acacia can also do this and indeed, while the Suez Canal was being dug in the 1860s, tap roots of acacia trees were found some 25 feet down in the deepest level of the cut. The sturdy little Aleppo pine struggles to keep alive in semi-desert conditions but seldom grows higher than 20 feet. This tree is a boon to nomadic tribes for its resin is used as a sort of chewing gum and also as a remedy for chest troubles. Its cones are eagerly sought because the oil they contain does not turn rancid if kept in the cone.

Recently the Tunisians decided to produce some of their own timber. They began by cutting down unusable trees and clearing large areas for replanting. The Aleppo pine was not considered in this instance for it takes 40 years to come to maturity. Instead the faster-growing eucalyptus was used and the Lombardy poplar. The latter, like the palm tree, has roots which will range further than most trees to seek moisture. Tebessa Forest is one of these schemes and has a quarter of a million pine trees. This is a joint effort with the Algerian authorities and lies along the border between both countries.

Each year the second Sunday in November is set as the date for a 'Tree Planting Day'. On this occasion the President plants a tree in Tunis and dignitaries in towns and villages do likewise.

There is a story of a young man who was staying in a new hotel and spent most of his time in the bar. He had many drinking sessions with another gentleman who was much older and also imbibed freely. The establishment was very comfortable but the garden had not been laid out and the building was surrounded by acres of sand. At lunch one day the young man appeared looking exceedingly pale. His elderly friend was solicitous. 'I missed you in the bar before lunch today,' he said. 'You look quite ill. What you need is a stiff drink.' 'I shall never have a cocktail again,' said the young man shaking his head. 'I had an experience last night that has cured me of drinking. When I went to bed I opened my window and looked out over the sand bare in the moonlight. I awoke later and felt cold so went over to the window to shut it. When I looked out the moonlight was still shining and believe it or not trees had grown up everywhere !'

What the young man did not realize was that, in a country where labour is still comparatively cheap and large numbers of men can be employed to achieve quick results, an avenue of trees had been planted overnight leading from the hotel entrance to the street.

Perhaps one of the most unique things about Tunisia is that, although small in area, it is a country of wide contrasts. As well as olive groves, vineyards and the fertile Medjerda valley, there is the strange lunar landscape of Matmata. Here an ancient desert people have lived for over 2,000 years the life of troglodytes in man-made underground dwellings. The stone in this part of the country is not substantial enough for building but is easy to excavate. A circular hole is dug, about 25 feet in diameter and of similar depth, which serves as a courtyard open to the sky. These are often very attractive, complete with leafy trees! Rooms, corridors and recesses are cut into the walls and connected by stairways to form a home. Stabling is also dug out for domestic animals and other recesses are made for fodder and storage. These strange dwellings protect the inhabitants against extremes of temperature and it is a way of life not only traditional but sensible. Many of these people stubbornly resist pleas from the authorities to move into ordinary houses.

The 'chotts' (salt lakes) and 'oueds' (river courses) have one thing in common – they are dry most of the year. The 'chotts', large shallow depressions, can be treacherous. Rain in the desert knows no moderation. Capricious and sometimes intense, it seems to bring too much water – or too little. If the former, the 'chotts' overflow rapidly and release uncontrollable water which can be disastrous. Fortunately this only occurs infrequently.

The 'Jerid' includes the lush oasis country between the Chott el Jerid and the Chott el Rharsa. Tunis itself is enclosed on two sides by water, to the east by the Lake of Tunis and to the south by Lake Sedjoumi. The northern part of the country is known as the 'Tell' (mountain) and from Sousse to Sfax, where the olive groves form a necklace along the rounded coastal area, is known as the 'Sahel' – an Arabic word meaning 'seashore'.

The southern island of Jerba, the famed lotus land of Ulysses, can be reached by a causeway from the mainland and again is completely different from other parts of the country. Its tiny capital Houmt Souk has an old Spanish fort dating from 1284 which adds charm to the small harbour. You can watch potters at work in the village of Guellala making their amphora-like water vessels. At certain times of the year you can go to Adjim, a coastal village, and see the fishermen diving expertly 70 feet or more to bring up sponges.

Also on Jerba are the two villages of Hara Kebira and Hara Srira, whose inhabitants are descendants of those who fled from Jerusalem when it was sacked by Titus in A.D. 70. These people are probably the oldest and purest Jewish community anywhere. The Ghriba synagogue becomes a centre of international pilgrimage every Easter.

Monastir, where President Bourguiba was born, was the Ruspina of Phoenician and Roman times and draws its name from a monastery built at the beginning of the Christian era on the site of the present town. Its ancient eighth-century fortress, the Ribat, houses an Islamic museum.

Tunisians themselves recognize that it is difficult to sum up the many facets of their country. One minister put it aptly when he remarked, 'Here we have no political or religious problems to make headlines. We are the Switzerland of North Africa.'

2. Tunis and Environs

To approach Tunis by air is an engaging experience. As you cross the turquoise Mediterranean and the fawn-coloured coastline scrolled with bays and inlets appears, stories of Carthage and her splendour come to mind; of her great circular harbour ringed with ionic columns where trading vessels constantly unloaded their wares and elephants plodded with the cargo towards large warehouses. What a fantastic sight it would have made from the air, for the Carthaginians employed artists, architects, sculptors and builders from Sicily, Greece and Egypt to make their city on the coast magnificent.

As your aircraft flies lower the Bay of Tunis gets larger and tiny white dots grow into buildings. In a few minutes you are skimming along the runway at Tunis-Carthage airport. Here, in the new £6 million terminal building, you do not have to walk for miles to reach the baggage carousels. There is no long wait to get a customs officer to attend to you, no mad rush to get on the right bus or catch an elusive taxi. The new building is intimate and friendly. With its small concourse and willing help through the reception stages, a welcoming atmosphere is created for the visitor – something not possible in the larger international airports.

It was opened by President Bourguiba in 1972. He became its first passenger by flying to his home town of Monastir to inaugurate there another new airport – Skanes-Monastir. Tunisia now has three international airports, the other, also recently developed, is on the island of Jerba in the south.

Tunis airport is a mere 5 miles from the city, which is divided like Budapest into the old city and the new. Its site is some 6 miles in from the sea and lies at the western end of a large lagoon, some 3 feet deep, known as the 'little sea' – 'El Bahira'. Like a jewel set in silver, Tunis is largely surrounded by water. La Goulette is the deep water port on the Bay of Tunis proper and, to save going all around the lake, it is connected to the city by a canal 20 feet deep dredged through the lagoon. The soil from this was thrown up to form a causeway carrying a road and railway which run on the coast from La Goulette to Carthage and La Marsa.

Modern Tunis, designed by the French, lies between the harbour and the Medina, which is the old part of the city and stretches to the remains of an ancient fortress. The population is some 700,000. The town is dominated to the north by a charming wooded hill, Belvedere Park, which overlooks the whole city.

The 'Kouba' of Belvedere, a charming blue and white pavilion which was moved there from the grounds of a palace in La Manouba, and reassembled in 1901, is a fine example of eighteenth-century Moslem art at its best. Ceilings and arches are of delicately carved stucco work, some studded with coloured glass through which the sun glints. Three sides have open galleries and the fourth leads into a small hall. The 'Kouba' is supported by marble pillars decorated with scrolled work and crescents, the sign of Islam, on the summits. Marble seats link the arches or line the walls and here sometimes you will see students writing or quietly studying their books. It is a restful place and from the entrance there is a surprisingly good view out over the city and the bay.

Belvedere Park itself covers about 100 acres and is criss-crossed with paths, bordered with eucalyptus, pine and palm trees. It is also possible to drive about the park. Flowering shrubs and hibiscus add colour to the roadside and there are benches where you can sit and admire the views. In the spring and early summer there is the scent of orange blossoms and jasmine. As well as the 'Kouba' which is a 'must', the park boasts a casino (closed when I was there), a small zoo and a football stadium – not to mention a miniature lake. Magnificently sited nearby with a commanding view over the city sprawls the air-conditioned Hilton Hotel with a swimming pool, shopping arcade, roof garden, coffee shop and night club. Your travellers' cheques cashed here will realize the same exchange as the city banks. The hotel was opened in 1967 and is only about ten minutes drive from the centre of the city. All rooms have a private balcony and the views from each are entrancing, especially when there is a full moon.

The Avenue Habib Bourguiba is the focal point in the modern part of Tunis and the neighbouring streets and avenues are laid out on the grid system. The capital has its traffic problems but parking is not yet impossible, just difficult! The best way for the newcomer to get his bearings is to walk first of all along the Avenue Bourguiba which stretches from the harbour to the Medina in a straight line. On your immediate right stands a high modern hotel, the Hotel du Lac, at the edge of Esplanade. It is built in an unusual fan shape spreading from a comparatively small base. Near here also is the Tunisian Tourist Office and the more traditional Carlton and Claridge Hotels. A double line of trees runs down the centre of the Avenue Bourguiba, giving the appearance of the Ramblas in Barcelona.

Further along on the left and dwarfing all other buildings stands the Hotel Africa, which is almost a small city in itself. The first six floors consist of shops, a cinema, a terrace with swimming pool, six bars decorated in different styles; one has 'English' decor and is called The Pub. A restaurant 'Les Caravaniers' with an extensive menu is on the fifth floor together with 'La Rose des Sables', a luxury coffee shop and snack bar. From the seventh to the eighteenth floor there are 170 air-conditioned bedrooms, all with bathrooms, radio and television. In the entrance there is a delightful fountain, on the first floor there is a commercial centre with smart boutiques known as the 'Village' and, to crown it all, at the top on the twentieth floor is the night club 'Etoile du Sud' overlooking the city.

Carrying along on the left-hand side from the Hotel Africa up the Avenue Bourguiba among the fashionable shops you come to the 'Centre de l'Artisanat'. This is a large shop in which you can choose from the entire range of Tunisian handmade crafts: carpets, stoles, all kinds of woven goods, carved wooden bowls, kaftans, tiles and many other enticing things including bird cages. Each large town in the country has one of these shops, the workmanship is excellent and, although things are not inexpensive, the prices are fixed and there is no bargaining. The Tunis Artisanat shop has strange opening hours. In the mornings nine-thirty to midday and in the afternoon three o'clock until seven in the evening.

Almost next door you come upon the Municipal Theatre, a lovely white building with steps leading down to the pavement where people like to sit as they do on the Spanish Steps in Rome. The flowers are not far away either, so the illusion of the Spanish Steps goes further. Just opposite in the centre of the boulevard and protected by trees there is a colourful flower market. Beyond the theatre you can glimpse the French Embassy behind a stately black wrought-iron fence decorated with gilded fleurs de lys. It was built in 1862.

Walking a little further along you come to the American Cultural Centre and beyond that a fountain plays in a shady courtyard with a café. Parts of the pavement are mosaiced in browns and creams and in some places it is arched overhead so that it is invariably cool. The Avenue Bourguiba now becomes the Avenue de France.

On the opposite side of the avenue there is the Cathedral of St Vincent de Paul and there are usually tourists standing among the flower stalls taking photographs of its gold mosaic-studded façade. If you do not cross the avenue you can stop at a café for a cooling drink and admire the jacaranda trees along the Rue Charles de Gaulle, which meets Avenue de France at this point on the south side. You can walk along it and shop at the Monoprix supermarket where the prices are not only marked but are far cheaper than anywhere else for such things as drink. Whisky and champagne are expensive but local brandy is far cheaper, and wines and local champagne are very reasonable.

But to get back to the Avenue de France. If you wander around the flower market you will notice that the double line of trees in the centre allows plenty of space for strolling. At sunset in the autumn masses of starlings swoop through the branches and fill the air with chatter as they do in London's Whitehall. As well as the numerous flower stalls, there are formal flower-beds set in this section of the promenade which are well shaded by the leafy trees.

The façade of the neo-gothic cathedral of St Vincent de Paul glints in the sunlight. It has a mural of Christ against a gilt background surrounded by angels, two with long, golden trumpets. This is surmounted by two towers culminating in domes, which have become part of the Tunis skyline.

Behind the cathedral there was once a cemetery but the coffins were removed to the Chapel of St Louis at Carthage. Among them was one of M. de Lesseps, father of the maker of the Suez Canal. Another famous grave, but this time in the Protestant cemetery of St George's Church, was of John Howard Payne, who wrote 'Home Sweet Home' and was the American Consul in Tunis. He died in 1852, but the body was disinterred many years ago and taken to a new tomb in Washington. A monument was set up to mark the spot.

Near the cathedral at number 43 is 'La Colisée', a high covered shopping precinct with many offices where you will find Swiss Air and Sabena. British Caledonian Airways, which provides a twice-weekly direct scheduled air service from London–Gatwick to Tunisia, also have their office here on Escalier D. Somehow it does not seem strange to see Caledonian air hostesses in their attractive tartan uniforms in this North African city. Perhaps this is because one of the night clubs advertised in 'La Colisée' is called 'Le Kilt' ! There is a large café with mosaic flooring, 'La Rotonde', in the centre of the ground floor of 'La Colisée', which is delightfully cool on a hot summer's day and a good place to meet in town. If you wish to shop you will find here all kinds of dress boutiques, beauty salons, chemists, newspaper, record and photography shops and a cinema, yet all within the same precinct.

Just past the French Embassy the Avenue Bourguiba ends in the Place de l'Indépendance but its direction is maintained for another quarter of a mile by the Avenue de France which runs into the Place de la Victoire. Here at the beginning of the Medina stands the British Embassy. This is in a way surprising since most other embassies, except the French, are out on the edges of the city. However it was built many years ago when the city was much smaller. Recent threats to drive the Avenue Bourguiba right through the Medina, happily, have been resisted.

Facing the entrance to the Medina through the ancient gate 'Bab el Bhar' or, to give it its more modern name, the Porte de France, it is as well to get your bearings before you plunge into the souks. On your right is the British Embassy and on the left another Tunisian Tourist Information Centre. It might be as well to pay a visit to the latter to get maps or seek advice.

If you go straight through the entrance you face the Rue Djamaa Ez-Zitouna. This is the main artery of the bazaar and if you continue along its length you will not get lost in the tiny side lanes. Once you have mastered this street you can be more daring and wander off on side excursions. If you lose your sense of direction inquire for the Great Mosque –Djamaa Ez-Zitouna – which is actually situated in the souk on the street named after it.

A short distance up the Rue Djamaa Ez-Zitouna to the left you will see visitors gathered around an engraver who specializes in hammering out tourists' names on little brass ashtrays. They are already decorated but there is always room for the name in any language you like. It is rather fascinating to see your name in Arabic. The engraver is called Habibi – which means 'darling' in Arabic – and often has a flower behind one ear. He is quite used to photographers and also usually wears a 'chechia', the traditional Tunisian headgear, which is neither skull cap nor a hat but a mixture of both. It does not hug the skull but is brimless and red like the fez and, again like the fez, sports a jaunty black silk tassel on top.

Along on the right at number 31 you will come to 'L'Orient Bazaar' owned by Ben Ghorbal Frères who specialize in carpets and all kinds of handmade Tunisian articles. They won a first prize at the Brussels Exhibition in 1958 and their leather things are beautifully wrought. For instance you can purchase leather book covers in different colours and sizes tooled in gilt, and their hand-bags are well finished and reasonable in price.

It has been said that the Rue Djamaa Ez-Zitouna should be called the Souk of Souvenir Shops. Certainly you seem to be able to buy practically anything along its length. The illusion of narrowness between the opposite facing stalls is heightened where the souk is roofed over. The passage way between teems with buyers and sellers. Beneath the noisy voices there is the constant frou-frou of sound as people brush by each other. Shelves and narrow counters are heaped high with household requisites, brightly coloured materials and kaftans, everything displayed in a showy way to attract the passer-by. There is constant quick-witted bargaining and although there is little or no room there is much flailing of arms. The shopkeepers enjoy bargaining and, if you are not used to it, the best idea is to decide exactly what any given article is worth to you. Start below that sum, as certainly the shop-keeper will mention a much higher price than he hopes to receive and then you can both meet somewhere in the middle.

Loiterers enjoy watching the brazier or the coppersmith. Fathers teach sons many trades and it is fascinating to see small hands twist and turn, carving, polishing or moulding fine silver wire into brooches and bracelets, or engraving intricate designs on such things as brass or copper trays.

The noise lessens as you approach the Great Mosque, the Djamaa Ez-Zitouna or Mosque of the Olive Tree, so called, it is said, because the founder taught his followers beneath the shade of an ancient olive tree on the actual site. The Mosque is also the home of an Islamic school where students learn Koranic law and philosophy. It is in the heart of the souks, which grew up around it. It was founded in the eighth century and its many domes and spacious court can be glimpsed from neighbouring alleyways. It has been restored many times but its large praying hall has kept its original structure and is not unlike that of the Great Mosque in Kairouan in that the many pillars, some Byzantine, were re-used from other ancient buildings. The beamed ceiling is hung with ornate Venetian chandeliers and the floor is covered with rush mattings. High cupboards flanking the intricately carved mihrab on the south wall contain priceless illuminated manuscripts. The mosque's 145-feet-high minaret was built in 1894.

I tried to visit the Great Mosque several times, as I have gone to such places in Middle Eastern countries before, but was always politely requested not to enter although I removed my shoes and was suitably dressed. I had not appreciated that non-Moslems are forbidden to go in. This is not always the case in other Tunisian towns but it is wise to be discreet and inquire if visitors are allowed. For instance, you can enter the Great Mosque in Kairouan although it is the most holy place in Tunisia and indeed the fourth most holy place in all Islam.

Although maps and guidebooks suggest many fascinating buildings to visit in the Medina, they are often difficult to locate as there is no space to stand back and try and glimpse turrets, minarets or domes from a distance to judge where you are. However you will find plenty to interest you. Shops and stalls are in close conglomeration and you never know whether, round the next corner, you will come upon some tawdry exhibition or something that will make you gasp with pleasure. It is the element of surprise which provides half the pleasure. The 'chechia' souk is close to the Great Mosque, and the cloth souk actually skirts one of its walls. The street which used to be the Slave Market is now the scent souk! It is known as the Souk El Attarine and also sells everything necessary for weddings. Small phials, filled with essences of flowers and other haunting fragrances, are held under your nose. You are assured that each is more exotic than the last, until you cannot make up your mind which essence you find most alluring.

There are too many souks to mention and some of the little frontless shops are closed in the evening with gaily painted wooden shutters. Vendors sell all kinds of food from sweetmeats to caviare. Once in the gold and silver souk it is difficult to leave. The silver filigree work is cheap but very pretty. The tracery patterns look fragile but are deceptively strong. Gold and silver jewellery is sold by weight, not necessarily by workmanship, so is usually much cheaper than in Europe. The souks are paved with flagstones and a gutter runs down the centre of the main alley ways to flush away refuse at night or cope with sudden rain showers. Everything is remarkably clean and the smell from the spice shops enticing. Beyond the Medina the Kasbah rises over the old town. This area contains government and administration offices.

The Museum of Islamic Art in the Rue de Château is not far from the Medina but is as quiet as the Medina is noisy. It is housed in a large palace, the Dar Hussein, which was the headquarters of the French military forces during the protectorate. A spacious courtyard is surrounded by tiled arcades, there is a fountain in the centre and birds twitter amongst orange and lemon trees. The palace halls are full of fascinating things from the past; illuminated korans and manuscripts, ceramics, coins, silken embroidered clothes, plaques and panels inlaid with mother-of-pearl and ivory, figurines in glass cases and lacelike stucco work some studded with stained glass.

There are other museums, including one of interest to philatelists; 29 Rue Es Sadikia which has collections of Tunisian stamps, first-day covers, and items from early postal days. Telephone and telegraph equipment show the advances made since 1888. Entrance is free and stamp collectors can ask for the newest editions at a special office in the museum.

The most outstanding museum and probably the best-known in Africa after that of Cairo is the Bardo. If your interest lies in this direction one visit will not suffice but at all events you must see it. It possesses some of the largest and finest Roman mosaics in the world, many of them fascinating ones of marine life. It was opened on 7 May 1888 in two rooms of the grandiose Bardo Palace. It has now overflowed into 40! Gifts were sent by collectors or purchased by well-wishers but most of the treasures come from archaeological excavations in Tunisia itself.

The Bardo Palace, at one time the residence of the Beys of Tunis, is a most elegant background for outstanding finds. Its great halls and galleries have tiled walls, painted and inlaid ceilings, carved and pierced stucco work and in one rectangular gallery, reminiscent of Granada's Alhambra Palace, painted

8 The tower guarding the arched entrance to Sidi bou Said

wooden pendants hanging from the vaulting like delicately formed stalactites.

On the ground floor the first room you enter has a sales counter with postcards, books, copies of some of the finds and plaster models of Dougga and other ancient Roman towns. This room and those following it have whitewashed walls and arches. Punic remains are artistically displayed in well-lit glass cases and on small shelves protruding from the walls. Light streams in from tall windows. There are grimacing Carthaginian masks made of baked clay, but more horrific than these is a stele, shaped like an obelisk, with carvings depicting the sacrificing of a child to the Goddess Tanit. Close to it stands a small Carthaginian burial urn of the type used for children's ashes. Also on the ground floor there are examples of early sarcophagi, funerary furniture and jewellery. Replicas can be bought of several stone friezes, one showing a row of cherubs holding flowers, wheat and grapes and others representing the four seasons of the year. There are many mosaics from early Christian times, one showing a man about to be attacked by four lions.

The shallow wide staircases up to the next floor have walls covered in large mosaics. Many of these have been cleverly filled in where pieces were missing. The galleries on the first floor also have walls hung with great mosaic pictures, and others seemingly stretch out for miles on the floors. Descriptions are in Arabic, French and English, which are helpful as the Roman numbering of the many entrances to galleries and halls is confusing.

Perhaps the most colourful gallery is the former banqueting hall of the harem which has a vividly painted and gilded medallion carved in the domed ceiling. The floor is roped off, except for a surrounding walkway, for a mosaic 1,465 square feet in area which was discovered at Sousse and has been relaid. It is called 'The Triumph of Neptune' and the God is seen in the centre driving his chariot pulled by sea horses. You can well believe that he had a marvellous golden palace under the sea with grottos lit with phosphorescent glow and decorated with corals and sea plants. He is surrounded by 56 pictures showing scenes from his fantastic life

9 *The ruins of Carthage*

beneath the waves. One is of his wife, the sea nymph Amphitrite, whose nude body is as rosy as a Rubens portrait. She wears a golden necklace and bracelets and her red-gold hair is held in place by a golden fillet. She is skimming through the water at great speed, her right arm encircling the neck of a fierce galloping sea tiger. Other pictures of Neptune's underwater life show sirens, centaurs and plump marine monsters. To add more riches there are display cases and, surveying the whole scene, is a large head of Jupiter set in a niche. The god's flowing hair mingles with his long beard. The head is from an enormous statue. The large feet, encased in sandals, are set on the floor above the Neptune mosaic.

The following hall has a large coloured and gilded medallion in the ceiling also. The walls are covered with mosaics, one being of two boats manned by fishermen. Various plump fish dart along the sea bottom but not in the least perturbed about being caught! So gallery after gallery have walls and floors covered in fascinating mosaic pictures of farms, hunting and more and more marine scenes. Before you leave the first floor for the second there is a small ante-chamber, Room xxvi, which has not only the usual mosaic pictures but a lone statue, perhaps not more than 2 feet high, of Hercules. Hercules, the strongest man on earth who wandered far and wide and never settled in any city, is seen in a compromising position. Perhaps the artist heard of Hercules boisterously drinking and singing in the palace where Alcestis lay dead. Hearing of this Hercules went out to seek Death, and wrestled with him and carried Alcestis back to her beloved Admetus. Although Hercules thus atoned for this misdemeanour, he is depicted in this statue simultaneously performing both an essential and an offensive action!

On the second floor the mosaics are larger, more artistic and utterly captivating. These fascinating pictures take you back to Roman villas, palaces, theatres and forums from Utica, El Djem, Carthage and other places. You have reached so far back into the past that it is almost with a shock that you step into the 'Mahdia Room'.

Fortunately at the entrance of the 'Mahdia Room' there is a

plaque which gives a résumé of the amazing finds. It appears that in June 1907 sponge divers were working in the sea some 3 miles off the harbour of Mahdia when they caught a glimpse of wreckage in 25 fathoms of water. Underwater excavations were organized and went on until 1913. The remains of an ancient slave ship were found to contain many interesting objects of marble, bronze and wood and other exciting spoils thought to have been plundered from Athens in 81 B.C. by the Roman dictator Sulla.

Some 60 pillars were brought up from the sea with ionic and Corinthian capitals, enormous beautifully decorated urns, statues and cornices. Among the bronze statues is a remarkably preserved second-century one of the winged Agon placing what appears to be a laurel wreath on his curly head. It has not been damaged in any way, yet other heads, such as that of the god Pan, have had their features partially obliterated. Parts of the wooden hull, some rigging and, perhaps most interesting of all, the anchor have also been rescued.

One section on the top floor of the Bardo houses a small Arabic palace with fretted stucco arches and ceramic panels. The ceilings are in semicircular patterns and much of the carved work set with stained glass. The sleeping quarters, with bed heaped high with brocades and cushions, is divided from the living area by charming alcoves and delicately carved 'mushrabia' screens studded with mother-of-pearl and ivory. The rooms in traditional style are clustered around a tiny central courtyard with a marble pool and fountain.

Display cases in this section are full of richly embroidered wearing apparel, marriage tunics oversewn with gold and silver thread, ceremonial robes and national costumes from different parts of the country. Marriage shoes with high platform soles seem strangely modern except that they are overlaid with silver. These enabled the bride to stand higher than her companions so that the wedding guests might see her.

Coin collections include golden dinars of the Aghlabid and Fatimid periods. There are also exquisite carpets from Kairouan, chiselled coppers, Kallaline ceramics with stylized lions, silver chests, gold and silver Bedouin jewellery, chased weapons and other Arabic objects.

The Bardo museum is about 2½ miles from the centre of Tunis on G.P. 7 shortly after it passes through the remains of the old Roman aqueduct from Zaghouan. The opening hours are 9–12 a.m., 2–5 p.m. in the winter and during the summer 3–6 p.m. The museum is closed on Mondays. Cameras are forbidden.

The former staterooms of the Bardo palace now house the Tunisian House of Assembly or Parliament and are not open to the general public. The entrance, up a flight of steps, is guarded by sentries with scimitars who wear scarlet uniforms with long white cloaks. The sentries are quite used to photographers.

Also about a quarter of a mile along G.P. 7 from the heart of Tunis you can visit a modern factory where there are handicraft workshops which supply many Artisanat shops in different towns. Here you can watch the craftsmen at work making birdcages, designing handpainted scarves and materials, weaving carpets, making toys and so on. You can buy direct from the factory and there is usually an excellent choice.

The environs of the city are as interesting as Tunis itself. The residential area of Carthage and La Marsa and the village of Sidi Bou Said lie some 9 miles to the north-east of Tunis and may be approached either by the Causeway, La Goulette and the road which follows the coast or out past the airport on a broad highway which is shorter and quicker. If you go the latter way you will see several signs to the right which lead to the American cemetery for all those killed in the North African campaign. It was completed in 1970 and is a peaceful spot with a marble pool overlooked by the white statue of a young woman in a flowing robe sheathing a sword, symbolic of peace. She is backed by a white plaque which reads 'Honour to them that trod the path of Honour'. To the left of the pool another but much larger plaque reads :

In this World War II cemetery, covering 27 acres, the use of which was granted in perpetuity by the people of Tunisia, rest 2,840 of the military Dead of the United States of America.

Most of these died in the landings in, and occupation of Morocco and Algeria, and the subsequent fighting which ended with the liberation of Tunisia and the capitulation of All Enemy Forces in North Africa. 234 headstones mark the graves of 'Unknown'.

Along the south wall of the terrace are inscribed the names of 3,724 Americans who gave their lives in the service of their country but whose remains were never recovered or identified, or who were buried at sea.

After World War I the American Battle Monuments Commission erected a memorial chapel in each of the eight military cemeteries in Europe as well as eleven battlefield monuments. At the end of Word War II seventeen military cemeteries were established, in fifteen of which a memorial was erected; each memorial contains a record in permanent graphic form of the achievement of the United States Armed Forces in that region.

The graves in these cemeteries number approximately 39 per cent of those originally buried. The remains of the other 61 per cent were returned home at the request of the next-of-kin. A white marble headstone marks each of the graves – a Star of David for those of Jewish faith, a Latin Cross for all others. At each of the memorials are inscribed the names of the Missing in that region.

An American Superintendent is stationed at this cemetery to give information and assistance. This cemetery is open from 8 a.m. to 6 p.m. 15th May to 15th September and during the remainder of the year from 8 a.m. to 5 p.m.

If you do not turn off right to the American Cemetery, or retrace your steps, you can carry on direct to La Marsa and its extension Gammarth, where a delightful curving beach, pretty blue and white villas and a few luxurious hotels make it a charming little resort. Its streets are lined with trees – many of them being the elegant araucaria conifer. Bougainvillaea sprawls over high white walls and through wrought-iron gates, fountains play in small squares and there are many tempting little shops. There are several embassy residences at La Marsa including the British one which was Alexander's headquarters towards the end of the Tunisian campaign.

A bronze plaque to the right of the entrance has the following inscription :

By the generous action of his Highness the Bey and the Tunisian Government, this property has been the Residence of His Britannic Majesty's Consul General in Tunisia since 1850. Here General the Honourable Sir Harold Alexander – later Field Marshal Viscount Alexander of Tunis – Deputy Commander in Chief of Allied Expeditionary Force, established his HQ after xviii Army Group under his command liberated Tunis on 7/May/1943.

Alexander said it was the most handsome mess the British Army ever had in North Africa. He himself lived in a caravan in the 12-acre garden, and tents were set up to add to the accommodation. Mr Harold Macmillan, then Resident Minister in Algiers, was the only civilian member of the mess and he also was loud in his praise of the beautiful villa, the Palais Ben Ayed.

It was built during the eighteenth century, white in Moorish style, with the foundation for a further wing. Seven arabesque arches shade an open marble terrace reached by curving shallow staircases on either side. You step under the lintel of the large entrance door into a splendid hall with colourful tiled walls, said to have come from the Bardo, and overhead the ceiling is hand-carved and brilliantly painted. Facing you on the far wall there is an enormous painting of a beautiful young woman on horseback wearing a plumed hat. It is the young Queen Victoria painted by Count d'Orsay. The hall leads on the right-hand side into the dining-room which formed part of the officers' mess in 1943. Again the ceiling is brightly painted.

If, instead of going into the dining-room, you turn left through an archway you see another portrait of great interest – that of

Sir Richard Wood. He has dark hair beginning to thin and is olive-skinned with a veiled, amused expression. Not everyone admired him. A leading French diplomat said Sir Richard's favourite weapons were 'ruse and pretence' but this may have been because he made it his business to further British interests and quell French influence! Unquestionably he was an adept diplomatist on Britain's behalf when dealing with the Bey, Mohammed es Sadok.

Richard Wood was born in Constantinople where he began his career. In 1841 he was appointed British Consul to Damascus. In 1856 he was given a similar post in Tunisia. In Turkey, where Palmerston sought to oust French influence, he had been an apt pupil. In Tunis he used similar tactics. Mohammed Bey, apprehensive about the intentions of France and Turkey towards his country, took advantage of their rivalry by turning to Great Britain for advice. Sir Richard shrewdly suggested that the country become a British protectorate and to this the Bey lent a willing ear.

The Beys of Tunis sometimes put buildings at the disposal of foreign consuls at La Marsa, where the court moved in the summer, but when Sir Richard arrived in 1855 the residence belonging to the former British Consul had been reclaimed by the Bey. The Foreign Office in London were less than helpful when Wood pointed out that he could not receive people if he did not have a suitable establishment and suggested that he should inform the Bey that he was 'not suitably lodged'. Just when he was tactfully doing this he had a stroke of good fortune. Ben Ayed, the Bey's treasurer, had fallen into disgrace and hurriedly went off to France. The Bey promptly confiscated his estates, one of which was the Palais Ben Ayed, and presented this to Sir Richard as a gift. It is still the British Residence! So Sir Richard moved into the charming Moorish villa which has remained the residence of Britain's representative rent-free for over a century, the only stipulation being that it should keep its 'artistic character'. The grounds are delightful with flowers, olive, orange and lemon groves.

It would be interesting to know how Sir Richard persuaded the Bey to add the new wing, but certainly he directed its construction, and this is where the official entertaining had always been done. The older part of the residence has an inner covered court with rooms opening on all four sides. One of these is a small beautifully proportioned reception room with a domed ceiling decorated with stylized cypresses and flowers in white and gilt, a similar design and painted with the same delicacy as the walls of the Berbers' Mosque in Kairouan.

One of Sir Richard Wood's first suggestions to the Bey was that a light railway should be constructed from Tunis to the residential area on the coast. Mohammed Bey agreed to this and an English company soon arrived to start the work. It was to stretch $21\frac{1}{2}$ miles from La Marsa to La Goulette and across the Bay of Tunis. In the days before cars Sir Richard Wood found this method of transport suited him very well as it ran close to the residence and, perhaps not surprisingly, it was found necessary to build a station close to the Palais Ben Ayed! It is told that when he wished to go to Tunis he could push a button in the residence which rang a bell at the station, whereupon a train would wait until he was aboard.

Like all beautiful historic dwellings there are many stories about the British Residence at La Marsa. Gardeners are always finding pieces of mosaic, shards or coins, but this is as nothing compared with a tale related by the British Consul, a Mr Johnson, who lived there from 1897 to 1899. He was resting in the garden one day idly watching a gardener ferrying water from a well while a blind-folded camel turned a water wheel. The man suddenly disappeared from view. He had fallen down a hole but, before anyone could rescue him, he miraculously emerged bearing treasure as if from Aladdin's cave – gold and silver coins and an antique Roman lamp.

Other tales hint at hidden passages, one stretching for three-quarters of a mile to a neighbouring palace. Only recently a French authority on ancient Tunisian palaces, M. Jacques Revault, while taking measurements in the basement for a book he is writing, discovered a space which he cannot account for. One wonders what this might reveal. One can say without doubt that the claim that the Palais ben Ayed in Tunisia is one of the most attractive British diplomatic residences in the world, must be true.

Among the La Marsa hotels there is one of the most exclusive in Tunisia – 'La Baie des Singes'. It is on a superb site and has 70 air-conditioned, well-appointed rooms and 67 bungalows with individual loggias set in trees – one of the latter with its own tiny bathing pool. A snack bar is conveniently near the main swimming pool. There are tennis courts and a private harbour for sailing and water skiing. Its discotheque, although in the grounds, is far enough away not to disturb those who like early nights. The situation is ideal overlooking the Baie des Singes, so named, it is said, because a nudist camp was set up near the shore some time ago and when the local fishermen caught glimpses of the devotees, one of them pointed to the beach and laughingly said to his companions, 'Without their clothes they look like a pack of monkeys!'

The hotel nestles in a 22-acre park gay with flower beds and mimosa. The main restaurant, on the first floor, faces out to sea and is of gourmet standard. Naturally there is a story behind the hotel and it is an engaging one. The patron, a Tunisian, and the manager, a Frenchman, created it together.

Aziz Boujema went to school in Lausanne and there he became great friends with Jacques Wolff whose father owned the well-known 'Golden Goat' at Eze – and still does. The boys shared rooms together for four years and then Jacques went to the Hotel School in Lausanne and Aziz returned to Tunisia. When Jacques completed his course he accepted a post as manager of an hotel in Guadaloupe in the French West Indies and handpicked a chef to go with him. A couple of years later when in France on holiday he fell in love with a very pretty dark-haired girl and proposed. He was accepted and among the wedding guests invited was Aziz. Aziz came over to France and the two friends were delighted to meet again. Before his return to Guadaloupe with his bride, Jacques and Aziz saw each other several times and Zizi, Jacques' pet name for his friend, said he had an idea to propose. It was that he, Zizi, should build an hotel in Tunisia for the discerning tourist and that Jacques should be the manager and supply the expertise.

The idea was thrashed out and Jacques agreed to come to Tunisia when his contract in Guadaloupe was finished.

A year later the two men met in Tunisia and decided that the Baie des Singes was an ideal place for the hotel they planned. The architects they chose were a Greek and a Swiss who had both lived in Tunisia for some time and knew the climate. Zizi and Jacques lived in the first bungalow that was built and oversaw the work as it progressed, like a captain watches his ship taking shape. In two years representatives of four countries, Tunisia, France, Greece and Switzerland, made La Baie des Singes Hotel become a reality and it has now been operating for five years.

Jacques, like so many hoteliers before him, knowing that one of the hallmarks of a luxury hotel is good food, invited the chef who was with him in Guadaloupe to join the staff, which he did, and there are few briks in Tunisia which are as light and crispy as those eaten at La Baie des Singes. Zizi and Jacques went through many traumas before their hotel was finished but the story has a happy ending – or should I say beginning? Together they have created an hotel which is unique in Tunisia and probably anywhere else in the Mediterranean. An easy 20-minute drive from the centre of Tunis, passing the airport on the way, on a quiet unspoiled part of the coast, yet sophisticated, well appointed and very welcoming.

Driving back to Tunis along the pleasant coastal road you can visit Sidi bou Said, Carthage and La Goulette. Should you prefer to take the little railway it has a frequent service back and forth between La Marsa and Place d'Afrique in Tunis. The stops going back from La Marsa are Sidi bou Said, Carthage/Amilcar, Carthage/Hannibal, Carthage/Salammbo, Le Kram and La Goulette.

Off to the right in La Marsa and clearly signed, with a commanding view towards Tunis and the airport, you will find the French military cemetery which is most impressive, especially if visited at sunset. In the centre there is a simple cross edged with rosemary with the grave of an unknown soldier. The inscription reads : 'Ici repose un soldat de l'armée Française mort au champ d'Honneur pendant la campagne de Tunisie. 1942–43'. Each of the many graves has a French army helmet at the head.

The number of foreign cemeteries in Tunisia – French, British, American and German – is indicative of the intensity of the campaign there in World War II when Tunisia once again played its historical role as a strategic cockpit.

The little village of Sidi bou Said is perched high on a cliff overlooking the bay of Tunis. It has both an oriental and Andalusian air and despite its modern villas and swimming pools has miraculously preserved its loveliness and character. From the distance it appears to float like a mirage on its rocky promontory, a maze of closely packed vivid blue and white houses curving upwards with minaret and lighthouse fingering the sky. Yet these closely massed houses have secret courtyards and terraces full of flowering shrubs, vines and garden beds. Bougainvillaea froths over white walls. As you climb the hills and see the villas individually each seems prettier than the last. Windows are hidden behind blue curved grill work. Balconies are enmeshed in the same wrought lattice work and always in the same bright blue. Not so the doorways, some encased in marble archways but they vary in colour and decorations are picked out in black-headed nails forming medallions, stylized trees, urns and scroll work. The round knockers are also decorated and some are in the shape of a woman's hand clasping an iron ball – the lucky hand of Fatima.

The main street is really a steep cobbled hill, the top of which is a flight of steps leading to the Café des Nattes where it is traditional to drink mint tea. You sit at little tables on an open terrace or on stone benches covered with rush matting and from here you see down the length of the hill. It is lined with small villas and tiny frontless shops. Flights of steps lead to terraces at different heights gay with pots of geraniums. Another open-air café can be seen down on the right. Among the gazing tourists there are very smartly dressed local people, for Sidi bou Said is not known as the Tunisian St Tropez without reason. In recent years it has become an artist's and writer's paradise and also a fashionable place to have a villa.

Altogether the village presents a delightful aspect to the visitor, if a trifle busy in the summer. Any new buildings are strictly controlled and required to conform with the overall pattern and, although it is possible for residents to take cars to their villas through the narrow hills, there is no way of driving through it. It is necessary to park in the places provided and thus the amenities remain reasonably unspoiled. However, you can drive to the little harbour, often gay with visiting yachts which snuggle at the foot of the promontory. It is approached by a separate road below the village passing the large modern Amilcar Hotel, edging the beach on the way.

Near Sidi bou Said railway station is a small, unusual factory for the making of the decorative wire bird cages for which Tunisia is famous. The bird cages originated in Sidi bou Said and the owner of the factory is Mr Samouda whose grandfather started the business. It is fascinating to visit this place, for the work is done by a few people in a series of tiny rooms and open courtyards smothered in flowers and tropical trees. The counter where your cage is wrapped up has autographs of many famous people including President Tito and Richard Gordon, the Apollo space pilot. Everything is hand done with simple tools from carpentry to the twisting of the wire which is cut, bent, shaped and twirled before being linked together like a jigsaw puzzle. The largest cage contains more than 20,000 separately worked lengths of wire; even the smallest will have 500 pieces. It takes two years to learn the craft. The spectacular birdcages have become so popular that craftsmen from Sidi bou Said are employed in England by a Tunisian Khaled Benattia (Lordben of Coleherne Road, Fulham) to make cages for sale in the United Kingdom. You can also order them from Sidi bou Said and have them sent by post. One American visitor was so thrilled with the birdcages that when he returned home he ordered 1,000 to be sent to his shop. The cages are attractive as lighting fixtures or flower holders and designs are many. The 'Sirocco' model is shaped like a lantern, 'Casbah' a domed light, 'Mosque', as the name implies comes complete with minaret. A favourite bird cage is one shaped like a balcony bulging outward at the bottom. It has two shelves inside, is used for spice bottles and costs about four dinars. It should be stressed that these bird cages are more ornamental than practical.

If from the Café des Nattes you do not go down the hill but carry on up, you will come to the delightful Dar Zarouk Hotel, a converted palace with a terrace overlooking the sea. If you walk beyond the Zarouk, which closes from March to December, you will come to a spiralling path with slender eucalyptus trees which debouches on to another terrace where again there is a café and you can sip mint tea with a topping of pine nuts and enjoy the panorama. No wonder Sidi bou Said is likened to places in the south of France and it is only the local style of dress and the calls of the muezzin from the minaret that remind you that you are on the other side of the Mediterranean.

Long ago Sidi bou Said was part of Carthage. Little stands of this ancient city with its legendary beauty and magnificence. You can catch glimpses of its ruins from the little railway but it stretches over many miles and perhaps the best way to explore it is using the first-class Hotel Reine Didon as a base where you can rest at intervals for a meal or cooling drinks or, if you have the time, spend a night or two and see everything at leisure.

The hotel is close to the ancient hill of Bosra which is 4,525 feet in circumference. It is the site where the citadel of Punic Carthage with several encircling lines of fortifications ruled supreme. Today it is bare save for a museum, and at its summit the spectacular modern Cathedral of St Louis can be seen for miles. It was built by Cardinal Lavigerie and consecrated to St Louis of France who died there during the Seventh Crusade in 1270. The Cardinal founded 'Les Pères Blancs', the religious order whose present members farm and make wine at Thibar.

The exterior of the cathedral is honey-coloured and there are two square towers. The interior, used as a museum since it was deconsecrated, is a strange mixture of western and oriental design. The nave is separated from the aisles by slender pillars with golden Ionic capitals and Carrara marble arabesque arches. Golden fleurs-de-lys blaze brightly against blue backgrounds behind the carved alabaster altars. The coats of arms of many famous French families are used as church decoration and memorials as in St John's Cathedral in Malta. The vaulting is brightly painted and the cupola is vividly blue with stained glass windows. Near the exit there are interesting Punic remains and Roman mosaics which do not seem incongruous in this unusual religious setting because nothing is crowded and the atmosphere is serene.

The museum to the left of the cathedral was at one time the living quarters of the White Fathers and, when I was there, it was closed because an upper storey was being added. The museum has a fine collection of Punic objects. However, the gardens were open and proved not only to be an outdoor museum but a delightful place to stroll. Wandering paths are edged with walls made up from ordinary concrete studded with sculptured relics of frieze work, chips of columns and other bric-à-brac from the Punic and Roman past. It is a novel idea to insert small pieces of ancient remains into something useful, for they can always be removed and in the meantime they are protected. There are rows of Punic stelae, broken fluted columns, capitals of different shapes, stone sarcophagi and amphorae. The distant past mingles with the present. Birds flutter in cypress trees, flower beds are well tended, bougainvillaea softens broken pieces of masonry. Many amphorae have modern Turkish cannon balls as stoppers! Headless statues stand among the trees and there is a recumbent statue of St Louis with page-boy haircut looking oddly twentieth-century. Excavations have revealed the remains of underground chambers. These are now open to the sky and choked with greenery.

Rather more than half a mile north west of St Louis' Cathedral are the huge cisterns of La Malga, a tiny village. During the Arab invasion there were as many as 24 covered reservoirs there. Southwest from La Malga and to the left of the road to Tunis, not much remains of a Roman amphitheatre which must have equalled in size Rome's Coliseum. However you can still see the arena and underground passages. One wonders how many Christians were torn to pieces by lions there.

If you make another start from the Reine Didon Hotel, named

after the Phoenician princess, also known as Elissa, who founded Carthage, you are surrounded by the most visited ruins of Carthage. A small hill by the hotel has several columns – indeed one is in the hotel garden. On the opposite side of the hotel the ruins stretch down to the sea but are so mutilated that it is disappointing and difficult to get an overall picture of what the city looked like. It must be remembered that Punic Carthage was utterly devastated and then sprinkled with salt so that nothing would grow in the soil. However there are numerous Roman remains. The theatre has been restored and is used for a festival each summer. It was from this theatre that Sir Winson Churchill gave a stirring speech of victory in 1943 at the end of the North African campaign. Close by there are vestiges of Roman villas. One has been restored and is used as a little museum. Here and there mosaic floors can be seen, many faded by the sun others protected by wooden covers. A miniature marble lion with curling mane roars at the foot of some steps and poses readily for photographers. The most beautiful mosaics have been removed to the Bardo museum and one that you can see there that has retained its colour in a remarkable way is of a sea-nymph swimming above a dolphin and surrounded by other sea creatures of Neptune's kingdom, including a horned cow. She has blonde hair and wears only golden bracelets, necklet, anklets and a small crown. She is clasping a rope from a wrecked ship. The sea varies in colour from deepest blue to pale green.

Looters have dragged away much of Roman Carthage but close to the seashore you can visit what remains of the imposing Baths of Antonius. One great Corinthian capital weighing, it is said, about four tons has been left where it fell on the ground. Another enormous capital, with perfectly sculptured acanthus leaves, has been placed in the centre of a roundabout at the end of the palm lined Queen Dido Avenue. It is floodlit at night and in its setting of green grass surely makes the most impressive of traffic islands!

From the terrace of the Reine Didon Hotel you can see the President's summer palace, which is the one used most often.

Formal gardens lead down to the beach and there are wrought-iron gates at the entrance.

The Punic ports are a short way down the coast. The original site of the naval and commercial harbours, although small today due to the depositing of silt, still retain their circular shape and give an excellent idea of how they must have appeared in ancient times.

La Goulette – the 'Gullet' – was an outpost of Carthage long ago and is the last stop the electric train, the TGM, makes before reaching Tunis. It is Tunisia's main port and is connected to the capital by a causeway across the shallow lake carrying a main road and the railway alongside a deep water canal. Except for the Kasbah at the end of the jetty and the main city gate, there is little in the modern warehouses, power station and industrial activity to remind you of its historical past. A free ferry leaves for Tunis every 15 minutes and the beach is very crowded during the summer. La Goulette's several small restaurants serve fresh red mullet, sole, bass and other mouth-watering fish which are landed in the fishing harbour. The main street is known as the 'Street with a Hundred Restaurants' – which is a slight exaggeration but shows how popular they have become.

10   *Stone lion at Carthage*

3. Food and Drink

The Tunisians delight in hospitality and their liberal reception of strangers as well as friends is proverbial. The guest is immediately offered something to drink or eat wherever he may go. In the desert the stranger is 'the guest of Allah' – even a potential enemy who requires shelter and food cannot be refused and once he has eaten his host's bread and salt, he may claim sanctuary. Eating together is almost a sacred rite. You will find this generosity from the richest to the poorest, and stories about food and feasting are many.

It is said that Ali, nephew of the prophet Mohammed, shared a meal with the Prophet's scribe Moawya. They were eating a chicken. Ali tore off the bird's two legs and offered them to Moawya who asked 'Was he an enemy during his life so that you attack him thus?' Ali quickly replied 'Was he a relative of yours that you think of him so solicitously?'

Tales of European discomfort when being offered a sheep's eye, considered a tasty morsel, at desert feasts, are numerous. There was the guest who slipped one in his breast pocket, forgot it and pulling his glasses out quickly, caused it to land with a plop in the middle of a huge caramel custard. My husband swears that if you close your eyes and pop it in your mouth pretending it is an oyster, it tastes delicious.

A moral from the Koran that 'haste is from the devil' proves, some say, that food should be carefully and slowly cooked. This is unquestionably true in the case of 'Koucha', a whole baby lamb seasoned and rolled in rosemary and inserted in a clay pot, sealed and then baked for some hours. When it is ready the pot is broken and an aromatic spicy smell emerges and the lamb itself is so tender it melts in the mouth. It is not wise to order this if it is not on the menu for it must marinate and cook for some hours. Also the flavour is far better if it is cooked out of doors and the pot has been buried in hot ash overnight. 'Koucha' is a speciality of the Reine Didon Hotel at Carthage.

Imported meats of all kinds can be had in hotels and restaurants, but the best local meat without doubt is lamb. Beef can be tough, veal is good but not plentiful and pork not popular in a Moslem country. But you cannot go wrong in choosing lamb or mutton. Otherwise select between fish or game.

The most popular main course everywhere is 'couscous', which takes much preparation and is delicious. Do not be discouraged because the main ingredient is semolina, for it is made with a difference and so far removed from memories of school meals that it does not even look the same. The semolina is sprinkled with water and a little oil, sifted and rolled into small grains, then cooked twice over the steam of a vegetable soup, absorbing its flavour. Chick-peas or beans are added to this soup. The prepared semolina has achieved such a reputation that sometimes it is even available in European food shops. There are supposed to be over 50 recipes for Tunisian 'couscous' but the basis is always fine-grained semolina. Pieces of cooked meat or fish are arranged around the heap of grains and then the whole is seasoned with mint and various spices. 'Harissa', a favourite spice always to be found on the table, is a mixture of dried red pepper, salt and garlic softened in oil. Tunisians use 'Harissa' with practically everything that is savoury but frequently offer Europeans a choice of really hot and a less vicious version. Approach the former with care.

'Couscous' can be served with a variety of vegetables. It is so versatile that it can also be made into a dessert by sweetening with sugar and adding pomegranates, raisins or dates.

Visitors returning from Tunisia argue that 'brik' is a rival of 'couscous' as a national dish. Undoubtedly it is far quicker to make even if more difficult to eat. It is thin, rolled-out dough folded around a raw egg, deep fried in boiling oil and served with a wedge of lemon. The white of the egg emerges firm, the yolk cooked but soft. There are a medley of 'briks'. The dough can be filled with small pieces of tunny plus the egg, parsley or other herbs, and the dough itself can be semi-circular in shape or pressed into a triangular envelope. Whatever the type the idea is to pick it up with nonchalance holding it at both ends in your fingers and bite into the middle where you can just discern the egg. You have to be careful that the egg yolk does not run down your chin. At least it is easier than using chopsticks because of course you use two hands! I have never met anyone who did not love 'briks' and the only problem if you wish to cook them at home is making the pastry, which is transparently thin. I got over this difficulty by buying three dozen circular pieces of pastry so thin that the weight was but a few ounces. As I flew home, I put them in my deep freeze within a few hours.

Before leaving the subject of eggs here is a recipe for another Tunisian dish which is easy to cook and rather unusual.

CHARCHOUKA

You need six small green pimentos, eight tomatoes, four eggs, butter or olive oil.

Remove the cores and seeds from the pimentos, and cut them in strips. Heat butter or a little olive oil in a shallow earthenware dish. In this, stew the pimentos and add the tomatoes, intact, when the pimentos are half cooked. Add a little salt and pepper. When the tomatoes have softened, break in the eggs, whole, and cover the dish until they are cooked. The Charchouka is now ready to be served.

If you wish a variation you can add a little cooked meat or minced chicken at the same time as the eggs. Sometimes Charchouka is cooked and served in individual egg dishes.

Whenever you see the word 'Mechoui' before lamb on a menu it merely means 'roasted'. 'Merguez' is a type of spiced sausage. 'Kebab' is lamb cut in one inch cubes, threaded on skewers and grilled over charcoal. There are many ways of cooking 'kebab' and here is the recipe for one of them.

LAMB KEBAB

Yield – 6 kebabs on skewers. Cooking time – about 15 minutes
Tomatoes
Onions
$1\frac{1}{2}$ lbs of lamb shoulder
$\frac{1}{2}$ cup of French dressing (made according to taste)

Cut lamb into one-inch cubes. Pour French dressing over the lamb, add a split clove, or garlic or onion juice if desired. Let stand at least one hour (or overnight in the refrigerator). Alternate lamb, tomatoes, onions on metal skewers. Allow space between for thorough cooking. Season with salt and pepper. Grill some three inches from source of heat for about 15 minutes. Turn to brown evenly. If you wish you can add mushrooms and bacon on the skewers.

'Tajine' is often used on festive days for such things as weddings and can be served either hot or cold. It is very filling. For ordinary occasions it has pieces of meat or chicken set in cheese or egg filling. Chickens are boiled, boned and chopped into small sections. Bread is soaked in milk and added to the chicken together with whipped whites of egg. The egg yolks are then added and placed in a baking dish. When the 'Tajine' has been cooked at a low temperature it is cut into small diamond shapes and decorated with lemon wedges and parsley.

Tunisia has some unusual salads. Salade Mechouia is a well-known appetizer cooked over an open charcoal fire and then served cold. It consists of grilled tomatoes, pimentos and onions which are minced and mixed with oil and spices into paste. This is attractively served with tuna fish, olives, hard boiled eggs and parsley. 'Salade Tunisienne' is a tasty concoction of diced peppers and tomatoes with tuna fish, hard boiled eggs, capers and celery, the whole tossed in olive oil and lemon juice.

A typical fisherman's dish, which is famous in many of the little restaurants in La Goulette, is grilled red mullet or sea bass garnished with fried peppers, potatoes and olives served with a side dish called 'Tastira' which is rather like Salade Mechouia. Pimentos, tomatoes and onions are grilled and minced and mixed with olive oil and spices and topped with a fried egg.

Local soups are always home-made and the fish ones are particularly delicious. The Arabic word for them is 'Shorba'. 'Shorba Bil Allouch' is a bedouin soup eaten during the winter and in particular when Ramadan has finished. It is vegetable soup with diced lamb and 'Harissa' added to taste.

Fish makes excellent eating and the fresh prawns, 'crevettes', from Sfax are delectable. Perch, bass, sole, mullet and bream, fresh and grilled cannot be beaten. Tuna fish can be had everywhere and is cheap in price. It is caught in season off Sidi Daoud where there is a canning factory. The lobster season starts in mid-May and closes in late September.

If you have ever travelled around the Middle East you will soon discover that aubergine, or eggplant, is the favourite vegetable. There are literally hundreds of ways of preparing it and, like the courgette, it is often stuffed with chopped vegetables, minced meat, herbs and other titbits.

Tunisian pastries are usually of the 'petit fours' variety made with flour, almond paste, ground hazel nuts and walnuts. 'Bouza' is a very filling cake, often too rich for European taste, and is made of sorghum, hazel nuts, toasted sesame seeds, milk and sugar. 'Baqlawa' however is very difficult to resist. It is made of many layers of paper-thin pastry with a filling of crushed nuts and honey between layers. Sugar syrup is poured over the mixture when it comes hot from the oven and this gives it an enticing transparency. In shops 'Baqlawa' is made in large square trays and then cut into diamond shapes. Most attractive also are dates stuffed with almond paste and other little 'petit fours'. You can eat them in the shop, take them back to your hotel or have boxes shipped home.

Many of the desserts are difficult to make when you get home but a particular Tunisian favourite called 'Breyes Beylicales' is quite easy to do and although it is time consuming it is delicious served cold.

BREYES BEYLICALES

Make a paste with ½ lb of fine semolina, 2 eggs, a pinch of salt and half a glass of water. Knead this into a stiff dough and roll out on a pastryboard until it is very thin – about a sixteenth of an inch.

Pound to a paste with an ounce of castor sugar a mixture of half an ounce each of almonds, walnuts, pistachio and pine nuts. These last are not often obtainable in Europe but can be replaced by using an extra ½ ounce of almonds.

Cut the semolina paste into two inch squares, put a teaspoonful of the nut mixture on each square, fold the paste over to form an envelope and deep fry. Drain them and place them in a dish in which you have prepared a little warm honey.

While on the subject of deep frying used in a number of Tunisian recipes, the oft-repeated instructions to heat the oil until it is just smoking or will brown a cube of bread in thirty seconds just does not work for me. There seems to be only one way to achieve the critical temperature needed for good results and that is to buy a cooking thermometer, keep it in the oil all the time and adhere strictly to the temperature recommended for the particular oil you are using. Do not try to cook too much at a time or you will cool the oil.

'Cassecroute' is sold from stalls like 'hot-dogs' in America, but you can buy the same thing from the food section of the 'Monoprix' shops in the various cities. It is a small scooped-out Arabic white loaf or bread roll filled with olives, capers, tunny fish and vegetable salad spiced with 'Harissa'. It is very tasty and a complete meal in itself.

Fresh fruit can be had all year round and for some reason oranges with the leaves still on them seem sweeter than those without. Pomegranates are an acquired taste but are extremely good when added to something else. For instance the flesh can be removed and mashed with sugar, lemon juice and a little rose water.

You will notice that many Tunisians, like the French, go home to lunch clutching a long, white loaf of bread, freshly baked, under their arms. Bottled mineral waters, again like the French, are very good and are sparkling or 'still'. Safia is tasteless and goes well with whisky or brandy. Two other well known makes which have a slight flavour are Ain Garci and Ain Oktor. All are rather expensive in hotels but cost only a few pence from shops and the bottles are returnable against a deposit.

You can find local beer in most places. It is served ice cold and is very good. There are two brands 'Stella' and 'Celtia'. 'Stella' is known as light ale and 'Celtia', which is more widely used by visitors, tastes like an excellent lager.

Tunisian wines are amongst the best produced in an Arab country. They are somewhat heavy and sweet with a higher than usual alcoholic content – 12 to 15 degrees. The Thibar Monastery, the 'Domaine de St Josef', produces more than three million bottles of wine a year, red, white and rosé. The white is pleasantly dry. The French Canadian monk in charge has been at the monastery for over 40 years and rejoices in the unusual name of Brother Romeo de l'Amoreux. Other well-known brands of wine are Haut-Mornag, Koudiat and Rossel. Then there is the white muscat wine of Kelibia. The aperitif 'Musca' has an apricot base. Most widely known and drunk is the firey 'Boukha' distilled from figs and not unlike akvavit to the taste. It is also equally strong and, even when diluted with iced Coca-Cola, it should not be taken lightly! Much smoother and most agreeable to the taste is the liqueur 'Thibarine', invented by the White Fathers of the Thibar Monastery, which many visitors think tastes like Drambuie.

Imported whisky, gin and brandy are very expensive in hotels and restaurants. Even in shops a bottle of whisky costs £4 or more and brandy and champagne are even more expensive. Local brandy and local champagne are about half the price of the imported brands.

Most devout Moslems do not drink wine or spirits because their religion forbids it. This is the reason you cannot be served with alcoholic drinks in certain cafés and restaurants. However, mint tea or coffee can be refreshing as a pick-me-up after sightseeing and the Tunisians make both well.

Mint tea is served in tall glasses with just the right amount of fresh mint but, if you are not over-fond of sugar, be sure to tell your waiter as Tunisians like it sweet. Again, if you do not like Turkish coffee say so, because you can have either 'French' coffee or 'instant' but Turkish is the true Arab drink and as strong and heartening as a cocktail.

The coffee purists insist that the beans be roasted over a charcoal fire and ground in a stone mortar. Usually one heaped teaspoonful of coffee and one of sugar is used per serving. The water and sugar are boiled together, then the coffee is added and stirred well. When it foams to the top of the tiny coffee container it is quickly removed from the flame until it subsides. The pot is put on the flame again until the same thing happens. It should 'boil up' three times in all. Then the coffee is ready to be served.

Coffee is drunk while still piping hot and it is poured into a very small cup. The grounds will have sunk to the bottom, so it is never stirred. You are not given a spoon so you will not be tempted to do this. From a full cup of coffee you drink half. The grounds may get in your mouth if you persist in trying to finish it.

Merchants will offer you coffee in their shops. Indeed wherever you go you are offered coffee although today a fruit drink or Coca-Cola may be substituted. You are brought your drink on a little tray and have it alone. Your host is not expected to join you. If he did he would be drinking all day and Turkish coffee is very strong. At one time it was considered a discourtesy for a guest to refuse this gesture of hospitality but, again, as you yourself may be visiting several places, it is not considered bad manners to refuse a drink if you do not want one.

4. Cap Bon, Nabeul and Hammamet

Cap Bon Peninsula divides the Gulf of Tunis from the Gulf of Hammamet. This finger of land 60 miles long and 20 wide is so fertile it is known as the Garden of Tunisia and is ringed with fine beaches. You cannot tour the entire circuit of Cap Bon by public transport although there are buses to Kelibia and also from Hammamet or Nabeul to and from Korbous. If you have a self-drive car the route, about 125 miles, is of great interest with little traffic. The rolling countryside is unbelievably lush, especially in the central part. At Beni Khalid the land is coated with acres and acres of vines sometimes fenced off by cactus. Fig trees grow in spread out clusters and everywhere you see olive, orange and lemon groves. Cereals thrive and you could think sometimes that you are driving through European farmland just before harvest time during a fabulous Indian summer.

Holiday opportunities are many and at Korbous, known for its radio-active springs (44–60°F.) with curative properties for ailments such as arthritis and skin diseases, a Beylical palace by the sea has been turned into a year-round thermal establishment. Sidi Rais, known for its wine, is close by.

Sidi Daoud has an attractive harbour but the tunny fishing season during May and June is not so attractive. Shoals of tuna fish appear during these months and fishermen use the same catching methods as those in Portugal and Sicily.

An enormous tunny net is laid from the shore out to sea, and should the running tuna try and avoid this they are frightened back to the main snare by well-placed fishing boats and smaller nets.

Great silver bodies flash through the air and the water, and the splashing enables the captain of the fleet to decide when to close in the net. The fishing boats, trailing the seaward end, close together, gradually drawing the net aboard their ships and thus enclosing the tuna in a decreasing semicircle. As the boats near the shore and the men pull on the nets, chanting and heaving, the tuna continually try to escape and flounder wildly with less and less room for manoeuvre. The noise increases as the fish leap and thrash into each other and their movements become the more frenzied as the net tightens. This in turn kindles excitement in the fishermen who chant as they pull, and at a given moment the signal for attack is given. The men plunge into the net among the tuna and the slaughter begins. The struggling, panting fish are stabbed and hit again and again and the foaming water turns red. The noise is deafening, the silver fish are covered in pink froth. The wounded, dying fish cease to fight and the enormous catch is dragged ashore and taken to the Sidi Daoud canning factory. This type of tunny fishing is often likened to bull fighting and tickets to watch from a launch can be obtained through the National Fisheries Office in Tunis, 26 Avenue de Paris. I do not enjoy bull fights and could not bring myself to witness the summer Tuna Fishing Festival. It is certainly not for those with weak stomachs.

Lying off the coast from Sidi Daoud are the islets of Zembra and Zambretta, the Aegimur islands of ancient times and a Berber outpost during the middle ages. Zembra has a headland 140 feet high and has facilities for skin diving and sailing. Boats can be hired from the fishery, in Sidi Daoud.

El Haouaria, near the end of the peninsula, is prettily wooded with pines, eucalyptus and acacias. Its disused quarries at one time provided stone for building both at Utica and Carthage. Nearby Cap Bon soars some 1,300 feet and its crannies are a favourite resting place for migrating birds. A slender lighthouse points to the sky further north and on clear days it is possible to see Sicily and the little island of Pantellaria less than 50 miles away.

Kelibia has the remains of a picturesque Hafsite castle built on rising ground. It looks very like a crusader castle with crenellated walls against the sky. The town was founded by the Sicilians before Christ but Scipio razed it at the same time as Carthage. Spaniards rebuilt it during the sixteenth century. Today, fishermen land mackerel and anchovies in its little port. If you enjoy fresh sardines none taste better than those prepared in Kelibia and there are a couple of hotels where you can have a fresh fish meal. An international festival of amateur films takes place here every July. The inhabitants export muscatel and raisins. Should you pass people with red hair and blue eyes these local people are known as 'Les Anglais' and are believed to be the descendants of British sailors from a wrecked ship off the coast many years ago.

Menzel Temime is a sleepy farming village some two miles from the sea. Korba is not far from Nabeul and is attractively sited on a hillside where there are some Roman remains from the days of the Emperor Augustus. The people here are renowned for their wool weaving, much of it done as a cottage industry. A trendy note is added by a nearby Club Méditerranée.

Nabeul, about an hour's drive from Tunis, is on the southern side of Cap Bon. It is famous for its pottery and wrought-iron work, which conjures up a picture of lines of factories but nothing could be further from the truth. The centre of the town is very pretty and one long street is given over to many little establishments, with a shop at the front, where a master potter carries on his trade with a number of apprentices. Tourists may wander in and out and watch the work from the soaking and kneading of clay to the firing and glazing of the finished product. Sometimes visitors are invited to sit at a wheel and try and 'throw' a lump of the soft malleable mixture and create a small vase. It is far more difficult than it looks and the leaning tower of Pisa is straighter than my particular effort! The coarse red clay is local but the fine white kaolin has to be imported. The designs for bowls and plates are traditional and pretty. Nabeul china cockerels are in all colours and sizes, and most people buy them in pairs. Few visitors leave the town without a parcel under their arms.

The less-skilled potters ply their trade opposite the big market-place in a maze of sketchy huts and kilns and turn out the clean cut amphora-shaped water carriers by the hundred. Ovens are fed with olive stones and olive wood and the smell is not unpleasant. The simple lines are delightful and I could not resist buying one although they are about two feet tall and a foot wide in the centre. I was with a party and other people followed suit. We felt that if they got broken on the way home less than 50p was at stake and although bulky they are not heavy. In the event I carried mine as hand luggage and was lucky enough to have a vacant seat next to me in the aircraft so I put it there and secured it with a seat belt! It arrived home safely, the fawn clay has since turned pink and I have been asked many times where I bought the elegant Greek urn!

Less than a mile from Nabeul, to the north-west at Dar Chaabane, the intricate stone tracery is made for the lovely screens, arches and windows that one sees all over the country. It is stencilled and then painstakingly cut through soft sandstone by chisel and needs a steady hand. This type of work has always been an Arabic craft and can be seen throughout the Middle East.

Nabeul forges turn out beautiful wrought-iron work, and examples of this can be seen in the local balconies and gates. Wrought-iron holders are inserted in the walls of buildings to hold flower pots. Most of the grille work is painted blue and, as usual, villas are gleaming white against which hibiscus, pointsettias, geraniums and bougainvillaea throw blotches of colour. Cypress trees stand stiff as sentries and in the main square many tile-decorated buildings add to the kaleidoscope. The Archaeological Gardens towards the sea have a few statues and pieces of masonry but the astonishing thing that strikes people is the enormous so-called 'potted' plant, which is a tall palm in a huge urn which must have been created around the base rather than the tree growing out of the pot!

In the main street, not for from Martyrs' Square, you will find an Artisan Shop where there is the usual guaranteed standard of workmanship in the crafts for sale and there is a discount of ten per cent when payments are made in sterling or dollars. Friday is market day and it is an occasion tinged with excitement. People pour into Nabeul from villages far away and the market place is like a vast 'Bring and Buy' sale. All kinds of flowers, fruit and vegetables make rainbow appearances. People mill about and watch auctions, and bargaining goes on with much gesticulation for gaudy materials, clothes, rugs and household goods.

It goes without saying that the most intriguing place for the visitor is the camel market, where the animals hold their heads in disdain while changing masters. Other livestock is bought and sold and bargaining reaches such fever point that one English visitor, without knowing what she was doing, bought a new-born lamb. It was placed in her arms and her husband, somewhat reluctantly, paid for the fluffy creature. It nuzzled its new owner and she found it adorable but suddenly realized that the British customs might disagree and, much to her husband's relief, gave the little creature to an old woman who had not been able to make her way into the melée. The latter hurried off with a broad smile plus her prize but whether she made the lamb a pet or cooked it for supper is uncertain! Suddenly it is time to pack up and go and within a few minutes it seems everyone has gone – the whole vast market place is empty and silent.

The district about Nabeul and Hammamet is known for its perfume distilleries and at certain times of year there is the haunting sweet smell of jasmine, roses and orange blossom. Oranges and lemons ripen the year around and in the spring there is the 'Orange Tree Festival' when the town assumes a carnival atmosphere and is 'en fête' for a whole week.

Hammamet, about seven miles from Nabeul and roughly an hour's drive from Tunis, is thought of by travellers as an unspoilt riviera. It has unrivalled sandy beaches and it is never too hot in summer or too cool in winter, a place where the hotels do not look like a concrete jungle and, as in Nabeul, the oranges and lemons grow throughout the year. Strange to tell, all this is true. Unlike the usual riviera there is plenty of room for everyone. The hotels are elaborately isolated so that each has a long uncluttered beach where swimming is inviting and, for those who prefer pools, every hotel seems to have one or two. For Americans who would like a Sheraton Hotel there is one – with all the name implies. As well as being surrounded by cypress and orange trees, yet adhering to the law that at Hammamet no hotel shall rise above a palm tree, the Sheraton sprawls in oriental style with hidden and unusual arched terraces.

Many of the Hammamet hotels have boutiques and they cater for various tastes and pockets. The majority have nightly dancing and floor shows and it is customary to go from one to the other. Discotheques include the Cleopatra, the Mexico Club, the Bedouin and the Miramar Club.

There is water skiing, sailing, mini golf, horse and camel riding as well as swimming, sun bathing or just lazing. Food is varied and menus differ but as a general rule you cannot choose badly if you pick local dishes, especially fish. To give an idea of dinner menus at random here is one from the Hotel Miramar, which has 140 bedrooms and 18 bungalows.

Bisque de Crevettes
Beignets de Courgettes
Soufflé au Fromage
Moules Marinières
Omelette Basquaise

*   *   *

Fricassée de Veau
Ballantine d'Agneau Sauce Menthe
Poulet à la Viennoise
Roastbeef Jardinière

*   *   *

Eclair au Chocolat
Pudding Custard
Coupe de Grenade
Yaourt

It is hard to differentiate between the many hotels and certainly impossible to describe all of them. I have stayed at Les Orangers which has 130 rooms on two floors, two pools, one of Olympic size, and it was very enjoyable, but others say the Miramar with its luxurious bungalows is for them. The Parc Plage is attractively situated close to the sea but has shady grounds and once a fortnight there are 'Folkloric' evenings. Most of the hotels are air-conditioned.

The International Cultural Centre gives open-air concerts and plays in its Roman-shaped theatre during the season. It has a most lovely setting in parkland. It is easy to see what care George Sebastion, the impresario, who welcomed many French writers and artists here between the wars, took when overseeing the planning of these gardens and the exquisite villa he built for himself. During the Tunisian campaign Rommel confiscated the villa and moved into it for a time. What good taste the General had! It is also told that, at the beginning of the North African campaign when he was striding towards Cairo, he planned to take over the famous Shepheard's Hotel there as his Headquarters!

Among the goldfinches, bee eaters and other exotic birds flashing through the trees at Hammamet are the hoopoes, their little coxcombs looking like tiny coronets set at jaunty angles, their variegated plumage vivid against the green branches. They particularly draw the eye because of their strange crests which rise from the forehead and are of broad feathers tipped with black and ivory. The hoopoe is about the size of a thrush with a slender bill and a golden-fawn neck and head. It is a bird long celebrated in Arabic tales. One fable has it that the hoopoe, also called King Solomon's crane, once did a great favour for King Solomon when all the other birds had refused. The King offered the hoopoe a wish. The hoopoe was delighted. 'Your Majesty, I would love a golden crown like yours.' 'Your wish is granted,' said the King. The hoopoe was pleased with his small golden coronet but the other birds were jealous and attacked him. His life became so miserable he had to go back to the King. 'Will you kindly remove the beautiful crown you gave to me,' requested the hoopoe. King

Solomon shook his head. 'No, I will not remove your crown but I can change it from gold to ordinary bird feathers.' The hoopoe was very grateful. 'Thank you, your Majesty', he said, 'I shall always bow my head before you', and from that day to this the hoopoe bows his head constantly and his little feathered crown remains intact.

Although Hammamet is such a well-known resort, there was originally and still is a fishing village some two miles away from the luxury hotels. Part of the wide beach edges a Medina with a square yellow kasbah. It is an enchanting little place where the inhabitants are used to tourists but still preserve their own way of life. Tiny houses with rough-cast walls are built facing inner courts and, being Tunisia, they have bright blue shutters, doorways and grille work. Most of the people live inside the medina, and the souk, although small, is full of useful things to buy – such as sponges which increase to twice their size when soaked in water. The region specializes in embroidery, lace and woollen stoles, and leather articles are good value.

The site of the Medina was chosen with as much care as knights would give when building a crusader castle. It is surrounded by a high wall and is hemmed in on one side by the sea, on another by a headland, the third has only the wall and the fourth overlooks a little fishing bay. The kasbah's open courtyard is reached by a flight of steps with no handrail and it is wise to keep close to the wall, although the many children playing here seem to come to no harm. From the courtyard more steps lead up to the ramparts, from which there is a splendid view. The curving sandy beach below is strewn with fishing nets and gaily painted boats and at sunset looks like an impressionist's painting.

The medina although not large contains all the things essential to village life. The mosque dates from the fifteenth century and has a yellow and white minaret the top of which is covered with coloured tiles. There is the hammam, turkish bath, in the tiny main square as well as many little workshops which supply the souk.

As well as the picturesque Medina there are several scenic drives

12   *The Medina at Hammamet*

from Hammamet, one being to Zaghouan, which is some 50 miles inland and about 35 miles from Tunis. Zaghouan is the place where Hadrian began his famous aqueduct to bring water to Carthage. Lines of these lofty single arches still remain in sections, useless and abandoned but mute witnesses to the power of ancient Rome. On the slopes of Mount Zaghouan, where the source of water began, are the remains of a nymphaeum, a stone reservoir, built with all the grace of a temple, in which water was collected. It is said that he who drinks of the Nile will return to Egypt, and the same legend has grown up about Zaghouan water. It is proverbial that he who drinks it will return to Tunisia.

About two miles further inland from Zaghouan situated in the fertile valley of the Oued Miliane you come to Thuburbo Maius. It has many Roman remains. The portico of the Petronii, built in A.D. 225, is still supported by intact pillars with acanthus capitals. There is a forum, a temple with an impressive flight of steps and various sanctuaries, more thermal baths and several dwellings paved with mosaic.

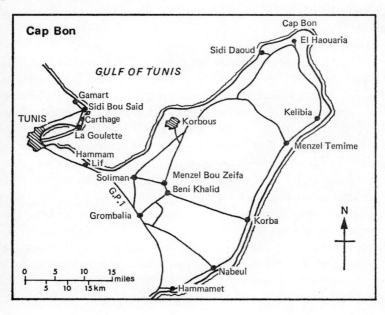

13 *The Ribat at Monastir*

5. Sousse, Monastir and Mahdia

Sousse, one of the country's most prosperous ports and its third largest city, is known affectionately as the 'Pearl of the Sahel'. Allied bombing destroyed much of the residential section in 1942–43. Since then the modern part of the town has been rebuilt, hotels have sprung up and western-style shopping streets with pavement cafés and restaurants edge towards the old city, part of which has been carefully restored. Commerce is not forgotten and exports include produce from the Sahel, salt, olive oil and alfa grass. An expanding industrial centre also has a car and lorry plant.

Sousse, with 70,000 inhabitants, is perched high on a hill with a sturdy ancient fortress overlooking the Gulf of Hammamet. Although 90 miles from the capital it is one of the liveliest resorts in Tunisia. The harbour, once a pirate's lair, is gay with pleasure craft, cargo ships, fishing boats from Malta and Italy as well as Arab dhows with their distinctive lateen sails. Sousse has an unusual appeal in that hotels can be in the centre of town, yet a stone's throw from a white sandy beach. The latter is some 12 miles long and if you dislike staying in a town on holiday the hotels string out along the shore far beyond.

For amusement at night there are discotheques such as the Topkapi in Avenue Bourguiba and the Loukala in the old town. Most hotels have their own dinner dances, night clubs or discotheques. Floorshows feature folk dancing, Arabic music and sometimes snake charmers. Many shops stay open until late at night and you can sit on shady pavements at open-air cafés sipping

Koudiat wine or ice-cold beer and watch the world go by. There is a Monoprix shop on Avenue Bourguiba like the one in Tunis. Most Tunisian towns have one of these, run on the same lines as those in France.

On the outskirts of Sousse are the famous catacombs, five miles of subterranean galleries where thousands of Christians were buried during the second and fourth centuries. These were discovered in 1888 and you can visit one which extends for over a mile. I am not overfond of wandering in an underground corridor but followed a guide in Indian file with other tourists along a narrow passageway. It was dark and very dank after the sunshine outside but our guide's candle burned brightly, which proved there must be some ventilation, so I was not unduly apprehensive although I felt happier when I reached the surface once more. Many of the skeletons are stacked in tiers and graves are said to be in the same state of preservation as their counterparts in Rome.

One of the charms of Sousse is the way the new rubs shoulders with the old. The old town does not have the same bustle and excitement as the new but is none the less captivating. Sousse was founded in the ninth century B.C. as Hadrumetum and is even older than Carthage. Hannibal fled here after Scipio had defeated him in 203 B.C. and its stout defences were razed by the Vandals in A.D. 434. The old town is surrounded by ramparts with gateways for entry, and the souks are always teaming with good natured people buying and selling. Everything is on display in the frontless shops : kaftans, leatherwork, pointed Arabian slippers, gold and silver jewellery, perfumes, sheepskin rugs and the eye-catching blue and white bird cages from Sidi bou Said. As you stroll around you can watch the saddle makers, carpet weavers and metal craftsmen beating and hammering. All Tunisian souks have a type of souvenir few can resist, called a 'Desert Rose'. No two are alike because they are not hand-made but created by desert winds from small pieces of rock. The winds cut into and remove layers of soft sand from the hard until only 'petals' are left around a small core. Sand roses vary in size and shape but are usually single although I have been fortunate enough to find two joined together. They can be picked up in the desert but, if bought in the souks, cost very little and are uncommon as gifts or to keep as souvenirs.

One side of the Old Town is dominated by the Great Mosque and the Ribat, a fortified monastery, which is the older of the two. The Ribat was manned by a type of dedicated 'warrior monk', not unlike a crusader, for his life was devoted to God and to save Islam from invaders – especially crusaders!

The Ribat, built in the 800s by the Aghlabites to protect the coast, had both men and women living in austere cells who vowed to keep the faith and if necessary die as martyrs. The gateway is most unusual, having been repaired many times with an assortment of filched pillars of varying periods and sizes. It is protected by a portcullis and leads through an entrance hall, also reinforced with various types of ancient Roman columns. The hall opens into a large inner arcaded courtyard lined with cells and, from this, two stone staircases lead up to more cells and you can climb a further 74 steps inside a watchtower which gives a marvellous view out over the town and was used for aircraft spotting during the last war.

Three cells close together have been turned into a little museum with exhibits of glass ware, coins and Fatimid ceramics. There are beautifully carved remnants of small pillars' capitals and a funeral inscription in the name of Hafsid Prince Mbarek, Persian miniatures and other charming oddments.

The Aghlabite Emir, Abou El Abbas Mohammed, built the Great Mosque during the ninth century. It is sturdy beyond belief, more like a fortress than a house of prayer. The rounded arches forming a cloister about the central open court are supported on short square pillars. Stylized Arabic inscriptions from the Koran decorate cornices in traditional fashion. The prayer hall, leading off the courtyard, has more graceful and slender arches and a handcarved wooden minbar but is of a later date. The floor is covered with rush mats. From the paved open courtyard a flight of wide steps leads up to the ramparts where the minaret makes up in girth what it lacks in height, but it has a pleasing dome. The staircase as in most mosques has no handrails. The public are not admitted to the ramparts but it is not a disappointment as the view cannot compare with that seen from the Ribat's high watchtower close by.

The kasbah on the far edge of the medina can be reached by car along a modern road and there is parking space by a clump of trees. It is dominated by a signal tower or lighthouse called Khalef-el-Fela and dates from A. D. 1088. The kasbah itself is high on a hillside and overlooks the souks. The museum it contains, although not as large as the Bardo or with such imposing galleries, nevertheless is most outstanding with some wonderful finds. There is no catalogue and you can easily get lost but the exhibits are interesting and many are annotated so that it does not matter. However, as I nearly missed three rooms which I did not know existed at the far end of the garden, the map in this book may be of help.

You go through the ticket entrance into an open court with several statues. If you turn left you will find yourself in an open courtyard with a pool surrounded by a colonnade. The entrance at the far end leads into a large hall which has some magnificent mosaics, two are dominated by the Gods Neptune and Bacchus. One depicts a smiling Neptune with trident aloft, riding his chariot pulled by galloping seahorses; the other a triumphant Bacchus in a chariot led by four leopards and accompanied by dancing figures. A third shows a scene below the sea full of an amazing variety of fish. If you return to the colonnade and go through the other passage which leads into further galleries there are two pleasing mosaic pictures, one of urns in various sizes and another of grapes spilling out of an urn which, when seen in slanting sunlight, looks like a silken rug. In the galleries on the south side there are several interesting maps which give a layout of the town and the governorates, the latter with archaeological sites. Also mosaics from Sousse itself and El Djem. There are Punic stelae and tombs. The garden beyond is full of flowers and trellis work covered with trailing blossoms and at the far side almost hidden from view there are three more halls. In the first there is a gigantic lion in mosaic and the outstanding mosaic in the second is a large calendar of the seasons. The third hall has a little dais from which you can admire the floor where, in vividly coloured mosaic work, you can watch a deerhunt. In an alcove on the right there is a large statue of Priapus, brutally censored in some past age.

You take Highway 82 southward along the harbour from Sousse to reach Monastir some 15 miles distant. The route passes a large salt lake cut off from the sea by a spit of land. Heaps of salt on the shore glisten like snow. You pass many flourishing olive groves before reaching fashionable Skanes which has several luxury hotels along the beach; Skanes Palace Hotel is opposite the small modern airport of Skanes-Monastir. The President's summer palace is not far away and you can visit the grounds if you get a permit from the Syndicat d'Initiative in Monastir.

Monastir itself is three miles beyond and is a quiet little harbour town but famous throughout Tunisia as the birthplace of President Bourguiba. It is built over the ancient site of Roman Ruspina, a base from which Caesar began his African campaign. During the eighth and ninth centuries Arab warrior monks built a Ribat, similar to but larger than the one in Sousse, to forestall invasion from the sea. Women were also part of this force and had their own quarters in the fortress. The Ribat is within battlemented walls with lines of cells and small square towers. Again as in Sousse there is a small Islamic museum with glass, pottery, coins and Koranic manuscripts. Son et lumiere presentations are given every summer. The Ribat's main watch tower, which has 87 steps, gives a wonderful view out over the town and the many cemeteries. These are crowded for Monastir is held to be a holy city and true believers from the Sahel wish to be laid to rest here. The warrior monks declared that : 'To be garrisoned for three days at Monastir opens the gates of Paradise.'

The women of Monastir often visit their family graves before dawn when those who have gone are believed to be lonely. The Moslem custom of sharing holidays and feast days with those who have died is a joyous one and on such occasions a whole family will join together and feast at a relative's tomb so that the departed may not feel forgotten.

It is worth crossing the causeway to the little island of Oustania to get an idea of the town layout. You can walk over in a few minutes or drive if you have a car. Though small there is a yacht club and café and from it you can see the Ribat and its impressive walls silhouetted against the sky. Close to its walls you can glimpse the tenth century Great Mosque affectionately called Bourguiba Mosque after the President. It is as well to stress here that the town contains this old mosque, the new one given by Bourguiba and his mausoleum all called by his name, otherwise it is easy to become confused. Added to this each town has its main street or avenue named after the President.

The modern part of Monastir clusters about the old with domes and minarets here and there. In the foreground there are several resort hotels. Pedestrian tunnels under the coastal boulevard lead from them out to the inviting three mile beach.

Across the square from the Ribat a path goes through austere lines of tombs to the Bourguiba Mausoleum built in 1963. The beautiful entrance gates, tiled in blue, overlook tree lined paths and two small identical arcaded buildings surmounted by domes. The gateway leads to an open court paved in marble with carved arches resting on slender pillars. The mausoleum has been built for the President and his body will rest in the imposing central domed chamber. It is decorated with tiling, carved stonework as fine as lace and stained glass windows. An enormous Venetian chandelier is suspended from the dome. The latter is encircled with a gallery lined in pillars of spiral design with plain capitals. The gallery walls are of pierced frieze work. In the adjoining chamber there are several simple tombs where members of the Bourguiba family are buried.

The fawn-coloured new mosque which Bourguiba has presented to the town was finished in 1966. The standard of workmanship proves that the modern Arab craftsmen have lost none of the skill of their forefathers. Certainly it is possible to see here what the older mosques must have been like before the ravages of time dulled the lustre and colour of their decorative work. The gleaming roseate pillars are a blend of pinks, blacks and whites such as the granite from Aswan in Upper Egypt, which was used for obelisks, temples and palaces throughout the Middle East, must have appeared during the Pharaonic times. You will see more of these granite pillars and columns in the Great Mosque of Kairouan, Carthage and other places but never in the lustrous hue as in the Bourguiba Mosque in Monastir. The inner courtyard lined with arcaded cloisters is edged with coloured tilework and stylized quotations from the Koran in gilded letters on a black frieze. The lovely fountain in the centre with four marble lions around it is strangely reminiscent of the Lion Court in Granada's Alhambra Palace. The nineteen intricately carved doors are of polished teak. In the prayer hall an enormous sparkling chandelier hangs from a blue painted dome and the 'mihrab', the niche facing Mecca, is studded with gilt mosaic and flanked by onyx pillars. The exterior of the mosque is colourful also; the arches are edged with blue, the fluted dome is white and the beige coloured minaret culminates in an edging of blue tilework near the summit.

Practically opposite the new Bourguiba Mosque in the same street there is an Artisanat Shop which has a large selection of handmade items and does a big business with tourists. Local people do their principal shopping in nearby Sousse and buses go there every hour. If they wish to go further afield there are trains from Sousse to Tunis every two hours.

Driving south along the coast to Mahdia some 30 miles further on you pass by innumerable olive trees many centuries old with gnarled trunks twisted into strange, antediluvian shapes. The route turns slightly inland to Moknine, a small market town, and then returns to the coast.

Mahdia, built out on a promontory, is a thriving fishing port with some 18,000 inhabitants. The busy canneries deal with olive oil as well as fish and specialize in sardines. The fishing port, gay with boats, draws people like a magnet. A note of glamour is added by the detached minaret of the Sidi Mteir Mosque which is of ornate design and decorated with multicoloured mosaic.

The so called 'Dark Entrance' is a windowless 200 foot long passage which leads into the souks. At one time it was guarded with portcullises and led into a fortress built by the Spaniards in 1554. Although there is no lighting, enough sunlight seeps through to enable you to see without the aid of a torch.

The Great Mosque was built originally in A.D. 921 by Obeid Allah but it has been greatly damaged and restored many times since then. Almost complete restoration work in recent years makes it seem strangely modern but it has been done with simplicity and good taste. Rounded archways edge the plain brick cloisters in the main courtyard off which there is an austere prayer hall with floor covered in rush mats.

At the entrance to the mosque there is a notice in different languages for visitors. The same notice appears at the entrance of some other mosques. These have become necessary because of unfortunate behaviour by tourists who do not dress discreetly, talk quietly or remove their shoes on entering a mosque. The latter is obligatory for Moslems. The notices are in English, French and German and give four points to remember.

1. The tourists may not visit the mosques during prayer times.
2. Mosque visits are forbidden to all those ladies or gentlemen not suitably dressed.
3. Visitors must not go inside the prayer halls.
4. Tourists may not go up minarets or pulpits and must not take photographs or touch the Koran.

Visitors will find some mosques completely closed to them, some are partly opened and in others they may wander around freely. The most beautiful and venerable Tunisian mosques are in the Holy city of Kairouan and by good fortune these are open to visitors. The reason for this is often asked and there are many answers, none of which may be the real one. One is that when the French arrived in Kairouan in 1881 they entered the mosques and this created a precedent. Another is that tourists have always behaved with restraint in Kairouan. A third that Moslems wished to show their most holy places to others who believed in God. Be that as it may it is a privilege discerning visitors enjoy and appreciate.

The main courtyard in Mahdia's Great Mosque had a catchment area for rainwater and in ancient times the water was conveyed to the nearby Kasbah by a series of containers on pulleys.

The great yellow Kasbah was built on the highest point of the peninsula and dates from the twelfth century. Its circular courtyard, where you can turn your car, is edged with remnants of Roman columns and ancient cannons. It is a good 100 feet above the sea and from it there is a splendid view overlooking the town and the fishing harbour. To the north-west over the ramparts you can glimpse the white headstones of a cemetery on a little headland.

Mahdia's name is an historic one. A Fatimite prince, a descendant of the Prophet Mohammed's daughter Fatima, was given the title 'El Mahdi' – 'He who is directed by God'. Having routed the ruler of Kairouan he rose to power quickly and made his headquarters on the rocky promontory which bears his name. El Mahdi's aim was to be Caliph of all Islam and, having quelled the surrounding countryside as well as Sicily, he set out to conquer Egypt and Syria. He left a loyal Berber clan behind him in Tunisia and in A.D. 973 realized his ambition, and moved to Cairo.

Some twenty years later Mahdia, secure from the land but defenceless from the sea, was invaded by various European powers and eventually became a lair for the infamous pirate Dragut. It was made a base for his many raids on Malta and her islands and there was nobody the Maltese feared more than this corsair. On one occasion he kidnapped almost the whole population of Gozo and then sold them to the slave markets! In 1550 Charles v captured Mahdia and laid waste the walls before departing, leaving much of it as we see it today.

There was great excitement in Mahdia when a sponge diver thought he caught sight of a hidden city on the sea bottom in 1907. Archaeological investigation proved that it was a large sunken Roman ship with spoil from Athens which had been wrecked off the coast in 81 B.C. It was nevertheless a gigantic find the results of which can be seen today in one of the upstairs galleries in the Bardo Museum in Tunis.

6. Kairouan, Sbeitla and Kasserine

Kairouan, renowned as the centre of the golden age of Islamic religion and culture, enthrals the visitor in the same way as Jerusalem. Like the latter it is enclosed behind warm golden walls and has minarets and domes of the same colour against a backdrop of bright blue sky. Thousands of pilgrims visit it each year for its sacred fame is known throughout Islam and four or more visits confer the same religious status as one visit to Mecca which enables a faithful disciple to be known as a hadj. The square in front of the Great Mosque on Holy days is said to hold 200,000 pilgrims. They arrive by camel, on horseback, in taxis and buses and either stay at a 'funduk' or caravanserai – small bare rooms around a large square where the animals are hobbled – or pitch their tents outside the town. For centuries the town was a rest place for caravans bringing gold from Nubia.

Kairouan is 97 miles from Tunis and 35 from Sousse. The route is an easy one from the latter by car and there are also half-day excursions by bus. You go along Highway G.P. 12 through rolling countryside. At the time of going to press the road worsened just before reaching the city where two 'chotts' flooded badly in 1969 and played havoc with it washing parts away and leaving silt behind. However it is passable and if you drive carefully no harm should come to the springs but it is as well to check on road conditions before starting. The unserviceable part of the roadway is forgotten, however, as you approach Kairouan which is on a slight rise and can be seen from quite a distance away. It has 89 mosques and their many minarets form a jagged skyline. These add to that created by fluted and plain domes all surmounted by three globes on slender spikes and the crenellated ramparts of the old town.

Just before entering Kairouan you will see a large map at a junction which is of great assistance in getting about. These maps are on most roads leading into the city so if you miss one you will see another. Once in Kairouan itself it is somewhat difficult to find your way about as many of the streets and the souks are not named or if they are it is mostly in Arabic. If you are not with a party you must obtain tickets to visit such places as the Great Mosque from the Syndicat d'Initiative in the Kasbah and the people there will explain how to find your way around or get you a licensed guide.

The story of the founding of the city is interesting. Some 40 years after the death of the Prophet Mohammed, one of his disciples Sidi Oqba ibn Nafi, was travelling by caravan in the desert. When he halted to rest, a spring of clear water arose miraculously from the sand at his feet. As he bent to drink he found floating in the water a golden goblet which he had lost in Mecca. He named the sacred place 'Kairouan' which is Arabic for 'caravan'. Like the spring itself the town came to life and it has become to Moslem believers the most Holy Place after Mecca, Medina and Jerusalem.

The Great Mosque is unique and the most sanctified place in Kairouan. It is the fifth or sixth mosque on the site and has been damaged several times, restored and redecorated. Being sturdily built it gives a feeling of security and defence. Its very large open courtyard is an oblong enclosure with the main axis running south-east. There are five domes and a massive square minaret of three storeys, the lowest of which measures 35 square feet at the base.

The walls of the minaret are over ten feet thick and the stairway to the top is not quite in the centre. There are three windows on the south-east from which you can see the central courtyard. The other sides have arrow slits through which the light penetrates. The steps, made of ancient gravestones, continue up through the second storey. They come out under the domed pavilion at the top from which you can see the whole town and the featureless plain which encircles it. The pavilion opens on to a terrace on all four sides by horseshoe arches flanked with a strange assortment of Roman pillars.

Pillars and blocks of masonry from antiquated buildings have been used for centuries to help establish new ones throughout the Middle East. Mosques and kasbahs are nearly always built on historic sites near ruins. First of all they were usually on strategic places and secondly of course the ruins could be utilized as building materials. It is most noticeable when kasbah walls are 'pinned' with Roman pillars.

The Aghlabites made full use of Roman stonework which is especially conspicuous if it is 'bossed' when each block is shaped to protrude slightly instead of being flat, or when blocks with latin inscriptions are set in upside down or sideways.

The courtyard of the Great Mosque is colonnaded on three sides with a porch on the fourth which leads into the prayer hall always described as having a 'forest of columns'. This is perfectly true for there is a miscellaneous collection of some 300 purloined ancient columns with every conceivable type of capital, not only of different periods and styles but of all types of stone – onyx, alabaster, porphyry, marble and granite. They vary in colour and it is tantalizing not to know their origin but the overall result is most effective. It is as though you are walking through different kinds of trees in a dream-woodland. There are 17 aisles with eight larger ones crossing them at right angles and the central nave is heightened by a cupola. It is ironical that just here it is said that, if a man cannot squeeze through the two pillars closest together, he will have overenjoyed the pleasures of food and will not enter the gates of Paradise!

The mihrab, decorated with marble panels and lustre tiles, is in horseshoe pattern with orange-red pillars either side. The cedar wood minbar, at a height of 18 feet, dates from the ninth century and is delicately carved. Many chandeliers with golden glass are suspended from the ceiling.

The arcades surrounding the courtyard on three sides date from the ninth to the thirteenth century and again are made from columns of many periods mostly with smooth sides but several are fluted. The great expanse open to the sky is paved with marble and blocks of stone set at a slight incline so that the rainwater can be collected in cisterns below a square marble basin in the centre. This is carved in such a way as to trap sand to prevent it flowing nto the cisterns with the rainwater. 'It is patterned in this way' said our guide, 'for the hooves of drinking animals such as camels, horses and donkeys.' Since the horse hoof patterns face outward and would not fit either a camel or a donkey's foot and the water flows straight into two holes in the centre without forming a pool I took this statement to be more folkloric than accurate. There is a gigantic sundial on a dais with steps leading up to it and also a complicated device used by the Arabs to record the seasons by means of the shadows cast by four vertical gnomons.

When I first visited the Great Mosque in 1970 scaffolding was everywhere and part of the interior flooring was being removed. As one workman strode by with a wheelbarrow full of rubble to throw away I saw a glint of green and rose and asked him in my smattering of Arabic what it was. He picked up the two pieces that I pointed out and offered them to me with a smile. They were tiny pieces of tiling. It was said then that restoration work would take several years but when I saw the mosque again in 1972 I could scarcely believe my eyes for the work was completed. The tombs nestling close to the outside of the walls, and there are many of these for it is the desire of numerous Moslems to be buried near such a sacred spot, are also in excellent repair.

Facing the Great Mosque there is a museum of Moslem art with ancient parchments, jewellery and ceramics. If you take the road running approximately north from the 'Pointe des Martyrs' at the south side of the old city to the Place de Tunis on the North Wall you can follow it easily as it is wide and metalled. The whole distance is only about 500 yards and about half way along it on your right on the east side you will find archways and alleys leading off. These are the real souks where you can see the weavers and artisans at work and bargain for their products. Walls in the alley-ways are hung with flower pots and singing caged birds. At night it is well lit and clean, the carpets and rugs are famous especially those in polychromatic variety.

Other mosques which must be seen are the Mosque of Sabres, the Mosque of Three Gates and, one of the most beautiful in North Africa – the Mosque of the Barber. The Mosque of the Sabres has a pleasing exterior with five fluted domes. It was built by Sidi Amor Abada and in this city of aged mosques it is this one, not a hundred years old, that has become a 'must' for tourists because they are challenged to perform a feat. Each visitor is invited to try and wrench a sabre which weighs 55 pounds from its scabbard. Although no one has yet managed to do this everyone tries.

Sidi Amor, a pious marabout (holy man) built it. He was renowned as a blacksmith and placed an anchor in the courtyard believed to be from the Ark on Mount Ararat, to anchor Kairouan to the same spot for eternity !

Sidi Amor presented many of the things he made to his mosque, several of which can be seen leaning against a carved screen. These include a gigantic smoking pipe, taller than a man and carved all over with inscriptions.

The mosque contains five tombs, three of which have the remains of Sidi Amor, his daughter and a servant. The other two are reserved for an Imam and his companion. The Imam will unsheath the sabre, thus protecting Islam and will complete an unfinished dome in the mosque vaulting.

The Mosque of the Three Gates is so called because of its unusual façade which has three arches framing three doors open-ing directly on the street. The arches are of slightly pointed horse-shoe form, like the dome bearing the arches of the Great Mosque. The spandrels are filled with palmette-like leaves set in loops formed by tendrils, but the top edge of this ornamentation has obviously been mutilated. Above this there are bands of decora-tion, set between four mouldings the first and third being Kufic inscriptions which record that the mosque was built in the ninth century and restored during the fifteenth. The cornice above rests on 25 corbels. The mosque's interior is a spacious, single hall supported by 16 Roman columns with brick vaulting.

The Mosque of Sidi Sahab, or Mosque of the Barber, which is outside the town walls to the north-west, is held in great veneration because he was one of Mohammed's companions and always carried three hairs of the Prophet's beard. When he died these were buried with him.

The Mosque has several beautiful courts and chambers lavishly decorated and the sun streams through stained glass. The elegant minaret is faced with pink tiles and surmounted by a gilded crescent. The opening to the left of the minaret goes into a 'Madrasah', a mosque and school combined; the archway on the opposite side of the minaret leads through a tiled hall to an open passage which gives access to an inner courtyard of great beauty. This forms the entrance to the shrine of the saint and has walls of multicoloured tilework depicting stylized cypress trees and flowers. These are surrounded by an arcade of polished marble pillars decorated with delicately pierced plaster work. The colonnade supports a painted wood entablature.

Off the courtyard there are alcoves and when I was there one was lavishly furnished and on a divan in the centre there were silver coins. A veiled woman in black robes sat cross legged on one of the many silken cushions and it was obvious she was collecting for some charity. I suddenly saw a cat sleeping on one of the cushions in a niche. The woman caught my eye and was about to wake it and shoo it away but I shook my head. 'Don't you remember what your Prophet did when he saw a sleeping cat?' I asked. She nodded and smiled. Mohammed is said to have cut off the sleeve of his cloak so as not to disturb a cat sleeping on it.

The Saint's tomb is in a domed alcove on the west side lined with tiles and decorated with stylized quotations from the Koran. There are numerous votive offerings brought by pilgrims including clusters of small hanging lamps beneath a large crystal chandelier. The tomb itself is covered with several silken and lamè draperies the top one being in gold over one of emerald green, the colour of

14 The Mosque of Sidi Sahab in Kairouan

Islam. Pilgrims sit in contemplative mood on priceless rugs and pray. It is peaceful and serene.

Less than a mile from the north gate of Kairouan known as the Bab Tunis there are two unusual circular cisterns called the Aghlabite pools. The smaller one receives its water from the Oued-Marj al-Lil when it is in flood, the rim of the basin being below the level of the oued. The smaller pool is connected to the larger one by a vaulted channel at the point where the two touch forming a gigantic figure of eight. Both are in fact polygonal and not truly circular, the smaller one having 17 sides buttressed at each angle while the larger one, 425 feet in diameter, has 48 sides of similar construction. The depth is 25 feet but the pools tend to silt up. It is a restful place to visit, especially at the end of a day's sightseeing. There is a car park, usually empty at this time. Birds wing in over the water from the nearby treeline at sunset.

The modern Aghlabite Hotel has captured the atmosphere of old Kairouan so completely it would be difficult once having seen it to stay elsewhere. Many of the 67 rooms and apartments are in two storeys running along both sides of a corridor with a long pool of fountains in the centre. The living accommodation is separated from the pool by an alcoved gallery on each side hung from floor to ceiling with the fine carpets of every hue for which the town is famous. At night antique brass lamps pierced and studded with stained glass spray the rugs with pin points of light and cast dark shadows on the ceiling. Skilful artists have decorated the wrought iron banisters with fierce looking Aghlabite warriors armed with sabres. Even the bedrooms take you back to the Aghlabite period with their barrel vaulted ceilings, leather brass studded doors and cupboards with handles made like tiny sabres. More Kairouan rugs cover the lounge floors and the food is good. One luncheon menu offered half sheep's heads and although the actual sight of these made me hurriedly choose something less spectacular, another guest assured me that the brains were delicious, the cheek tasty and he wished there was a whole tongue instead of half !

From Kairouan to Sbeitla you take the G.P. 3 Highway out of the town and Kasserine is some 18 miles further on.

15   *The Roman amphitheatre at El Djem*

Sbeitla is a small place of 4,000 inhabitants and is famous for the ruins of the Roman city of Sufetula which are just on its outskirts. You will pass them on your right as you leave by Highway G.P. 13 for Kasserine. They are wired in and cover a large area some 4,000 yards long and 1,630 yards wide. At the end nearest the town, and on a slight rise very close to the road, stands the third century Diocletian Triumphal Arch which has been restored. With its great honey coloured blocks and slender Corinthian columns emphasized by the surrounding green trees, it makes a dramatic picture against the blue sky. The columns have capitals wreathed with scrolled acanthus leaves which might have been sculptured yesterday.

Sufetula was a capital city independent of Carthage at the beginning of the seventh century and, although today the whole site is strewn with pieces of masonry which it is hoped will be pieced together one day, there are several buildings still standing. There are Christian Basilicas, Byzantine fortresses, small Roman baths with fish mosaics (which are near the entrance) and a Forum, encircled by a 13-foot wall, paved and measuring 720 yards by 840.

The ruins of three important temples, built on a raised platform, survive close to the Forum. These were dedicated to Juno, Jupiter and Minerva, a virgin goddess who gave her patronage to literature. When a Roman poet's verse would not flow smoothly he would appeal to Minerva for inspiration. It is hoped that theatrical performances similar to those in Dougga will soon be put on at Sbeitla during the summer.

Kasserine has a present population of about 9,000 and is an important centre for alfa grass which grows in the region and there is a processing plant for extracting cellulose from it. Part of the town has risen over the site of Cillium and there are a number of Roman ruins including a triumphal arch and sections of an aqueduct. The town is at an altitude of 2,200 feet and Tunisia's highest mountain, the Djebel Chambi some 5,100 feet high, is not far away. You can drive over an indifferent road to the lower slopes and the views are worth it. This is hunting country and there are wild boar, hares and partridges.

7. El Djem, Sfax and the Kerkenna Islands

Wherever Roman civilization conquered it left an imperishable stamp in the monuments it raised. All the great amphitheatres were designed in imitation of the Colosseum in Rome although they differ one from the other in details of construction. Of these the most outstanding is El Djem, all that remains of ancient Thysdrus.

The first glimpse you get of El Djem is as exciting and surprising as seeing the Great Pyramid for the first time. It appears on the horizon of a featureless plain like a gigantic ship on an expanse of ocean. It is of tremendous size, the more impressive because in the distance it appears to be in complete isolation. As you draw closer and it becomes larger you realize that this mighty edifice, second in size only to the Colosseum in Rome, is aproned by an Arab town of 10,000 inhabitants. Built of limestone about A.D. 240 it consists of three arcades topped by a fourth storey of windows; the first and third arcades are Corinthian; the middle composite. On one side the wall has been largely removed probably by later builders in search of material. Its measurements give the best idea of size. Along its greatest axis it is 488 feet and along the shortest 406. The arena itself is 300 feet long and the galleries are 60 feet wide.

The staunch nature of the building can be judged by its amazing preservation when everything else of Thysdrus has completely disappeared. It is difficult to understand the fascination that gladiatorial fights to the death or the spectacle of humans being torn to pieces by lions, held for the Romans. Yet it was so and the remains of such magnificent amphitheatres as those in Verona,

Pola, Arles, Nimes and El Djem prove that the sport was not only enjoyed in Rome.

St Augustine is said to have related the following tale of El Djem. A friend of his, one Alipuis by name, was persuaded to go to the amphitheatre on a big feast day. He was reluctant to do so and determined to keep his eyes closed during the afternoon's sport. However the shouting, screaming and general noise was so great that he opened his eyes and looked – looked and was lost. Although horrified at what he saw he was also fascinated and could not stop watching and then he found he was shouting until he was hoarse like everyone else. Later he tried to stifle his desire to go again but when the next show was put on he went and had to admit that he actually enjoyed watching human beings struggling with frenzied beasts and that the smell of warm blood was intoxicating. So, like thousands of others, Alipius became an aficionado of El Djem.

El Djem rises to a height of 120 feet and could hold 30,000 spectators. Two galleries beneath the floor of the arena are in the form of a cross and it is said that a statue of Marcus Aurelius stood in the centre of one and when the gladiators left their chambers to fight they marched to right and to left around the figure before entering the arena.

Today no sense of past horror survives. The sprawling gigantic building has been baked by time and the sun to a lovely honey colour, as so many other ancient buildings in Tunisia. Birds wing merrily through the arches and nest in the broken capitals – the sun lights your way up and down steps and the lofty galleries. It is a place to sit and dream either in the warmth of the sun or in cool shade. The size of the amphitheatre is staggering from any angle for El Djem is the largest Roman monument in North Africa. Walking in some places is treacherous and parts are barricaded where the floor is really dangerous. The views into the arena itself from the archways and embrasures are awe inspiring and the imagination can run riot when remembering the ghastly scenes that took place there in the name of amusement.

El Djem did not serve only as a theatre. Its most famous moment came when it was used as a fortress during the Hilalian invasion. The story of the famous Queen Kahena is reminiscent of that of Queen Zenobia. Zenobia had exercised great sway over a Palmyrene-Bedouin army in Syria when Palmyra reached its peak of greatness in A.D. 270. Her beauty and prestige were by-words. The amazing ruins of Palmyra are a lasting reminder of her prowess when, as Queen of the desert city, she ruled an empire and sought to conquer Rome. Queen Kahena also led a victorious army. She first became leader of several Berber tribes and by her diplomacy she made them forget their local rivalries and band together behind her. She then led them in revolt against Carthage and won the day. El Djem became her headquarters and was turned into a fortress.

Like Zenobia, Kahena was renowned for her beauty and was wooed by many Berber Princes but she rejected them all. The most powerful Prince, who had the ear of many of her subjects, was not only debauched and evil but also ugly and had many wives. He demanded her hand and was so insistent that she pretended to love him, but in secret made plans for his removal. She acquiesced to his pleas of love and, when he visited her apartments and was about to claim her, she pulled a dagger from her robes and stabbed him.

Subsequently Kahena became even more powerful and led a series of successful campaigns, always returning to El Djem in triumph. In A.D. 703 the Moslems, led by General Hassan, swore to bring Kahena to her knees. Fortunes changed and she suffered defeat after defeat but still retained El Djem, Hassan beseiged the great fortress. Kahena and her retainers withstood this for a year. When her forces could hold out no longer they begged her to go into hiding but she would not leave El Djem. When all was lost, rather than be captured, she plunged her own sword into her breast. General Hassan was not appeased by this gesture and ordered her head cut off. He sent it in a casket, studded with jewels, as a token of fidelity to the Caliph in Bagdad.

Sfax is some 40 miles from El Djem and before you reach this, the second largest town in Tunisia, you pass through olive grove after olive grove. In the sunny weather the trees cast pools of shadow in slanting lines, their silvery leaves cool against the yellow sand. As you draw closer to the coast they seem to flourish even more, perhaps because the olive has a marked partiality to sea breezes.

The olive was introduced along the North African coast by the Phoenicians and has been a boon ever since. The Roman at home and abroad knew its value and the wealthy not only used it for food but also as an adjunct to the toilet. A Roman thought that long and pleasant life depended on two fluids – 'Wine within and oil without'.

Although the olive made up such a great part of the Tunisian farmer's life it was a precarious one because of little attention. Large untended trees produced sporadic luxuriant harvests but seldom two years running. Also the harvesting of the fruit was done on a haphazard basis either awaiting the convenience of the owner to shake it down or for it to drop naturally when it often lay too long on the ground. Since the French brought their expertise to the country the harvest has ceased to be a hit or miss affair. Whole plantations have trees the same size and are regimented in long lines like platoons. Grafting, propagation, pruning and seeking the best soil is as important for the olive, say the French, as for the grape. Strangely enough the varieties of olive known to the modern cultivator exceed those of the vine.

Sfax is not only known for its encircling olive groves but also for its treatment and export of phosphates. It has a large fish industry and specializes in octopus and sponge diving. In the Second World War it suffered much damage from Allied aircraft when held by the Germans and on the southern outskirts of the town there is another war cemetery.

The modern part is charming; not too big to stroll around but with well spaced out white buildings and palm lined boulevards, little squares and fountains. It reminds one of Tunis but on a much smaller scale, and the railway, coming from the west bringing the phosphates from Metlaoui and Redevef, has a convenient station at the end of Avenue Bourguiba. Ronald Firbank is quoted as saying that Sfax is the most beautiful city in the world. Certainly it has a sophisticated atmosphere all its own and is ringed about with white villas and well kept gardens. Avenue Bourguiba, a smaller edition of the one in Tunis, has attractive buildings and several smart eating places like the Café de la Paix and the Hotel Mabrouk. One of the most engaging things about Sfax is that you can reach most places in the centre within a few minutes walk. The Municipal Theatre is in the Boulevard de la République. This avenue is arcaded and is a delightful place to shop or stop for a cooling drink on a hot sunny day. In the Place Hedi Chaker you come upon the Municipal building with its slender clock tower. It also houses a regional museum which has some wonderful Roman mosaics from the south of Sfax. In the same building you will find an Information Office where the staff are most helpful although they did not know the answer to my olive branch question.

I was very curious to know why olive branches were secured in a semi-circle on the walls of many buildings including the post office. I asked people what it meant and there were several answers. Perhaps one day I shall know the real one. Most people looked surprised and said, 'I don't know but we have always done it.' 'Well,' said another, 'the leaves of the olive tree keep insects away – so my father told me when I asked him as a child.'

'But the leaves dry so quickly that cannot be possible,' I replied quickly. My informant looked puzzled and shrugged his shoulders.

'It brings good fortune,' the porter of our hotel said. The barman had another reply, 'It keeps illness and the "afreets" (evil demons) away.'

Whatever the reason there are enough dried olive branches on the buildings of Sfax to start a new olive grove. Even the hotel where we stayed, which was a charming old fashioned Victorian type of place with excellent food, not only had the dried olive branches on its outside wall but was named 'The Olives'.

In sharp contrast to the pleasant gardens and lackadaisical pavement café life in the centre of town, you can visit the lively fishing port with its hundreds of ships or shop and bargain in the labyrinth of the Medina. Sfax's crenellated Medina walls and ramparts are ninth century, the same date as the Great Mosque which rises from the centre of the Medina and is said to have the most beautiful minaret in the country. It has three storeys like the Great Mosque in Kairouan but there the likeness ends for it is slender and richly sculptured. Two of the most picturesque souks, those of the 'Jewellers' and 'Dyers', are cheek by jowl with the mosque. A place not to be missed in the Medina is an 18th century palace, the Dar Djellouil, which has been turned into a folk museum. Among the fascinating items are richly embroidered wedding clothes, jewellery and stills for extracting scent essences from flowers since Sfax is also known for its perfumes. The palace itself is enchanting with an open courtyard in the centre.

You may hire a boat at the harbour and reach the attractive islands of the Kerkenna Archipelago some 12 miles away in a leisurely three hours or you can take the ferry which goes twice a day and carries a few cars. The trip takes under the hour. On arrival a car service connects the port of disembarkation, Sidi Youssef, with the villages. The two main islands are Chergui and Gharbi, Gharbi, the southernmost, is eight miles long and four-and-a-half miles wide. The two islands are connected by a causeway first built by the Romans. The sea surrounding the islands is very shallow and at low tide the sand stretches out a good distance. This has caused the evolution of a special type of flat bottomed boat to avoid running aground known as a 'loude'.

The Kerkenna Islands have a Polynesian atmosphere. Most of the 15,000 people are fisherfolk. They catch fish as their fathers did before them, by setting up palm frond fences on the shelving beaches which trap the fish as the tide recedes so that they fall into waiting nets. This has something in common with the system used in the Bay of Fundy in Canada, the only place I know where fishing is done by horse and cart. Nets are strung between tall poles above the low water line and, when the tide goes out, the fishermen drive along the beach raking the fish out of the nets. The other method used in the Kerkenna islands is also carried out in many other parts of the Middle East, it is to beat the water when fish are about, thus frightening them into trailing nets. Octopus are caught by hand in specially hollowed out rocks where they try to hide.

The flat islands of Kerkenna have pretty indented shore lines and are covered by half a million palm trees. You can motor along the main road which traverses the islands but side roads are little more than tracks. The atmosphere is lazy and peaceful and at sunset the tall palm trees are reflected in the water and the sky and sea are drenched in rainbow colours. Such mundane things as telephones, trains and aircraft seem a million miles away and for once time does not seem to matter. With today's pressure on holiday spaces in the sunny Mediterranean, one wonders how long they can escape the eye of the developers and remain unspoiled.

There are about a dozen villages and you will see esparto grass baskets, ropes and olive press filters drying in the sun everywhere for the twisting and braiding of this fibre is part of the day's work for every housewife. It is said in the islands that 'A house without esparto grass is an empty house'. The palm tree is also part of the Kerkennian's way of life for it provides traps for the fishing grounds, fuel for cooking, wood for building – not to mention dates for food and palm 'toddy' called 'lagmi' that is claimed to taste like barley water but certainly has a different effect.

Beneath the palm fronds' shade animals browse, fig trees and vegetables flourish, men mend their fishing nets, women do embroidery, which is a local craft, or twist and braid esparto grass and divers sort out their sponges by sizes for the souks on the mainland. It is a purposeful yet tranquil life until there is a festival, wedding or circumcision celebration. The local people are tourist conscious and do not object to visitors watching their festivities especially weddings, which are great occasions for dressing up, dancing and feasting.

There is a small hotel called the Cercinna which has thatched huts or the Kerkenna Hotel on Sidi Frey Beach which is air-conditioned and has 98 rooms. The beaches are good but the shallow water means you have to walk out quite a way before you can take a dip.

Islands always remind me of exiles and Kerkenna has had many. Successive Beys sent their unwanted wives there. Hannibal fled to the islands after the Battle of Zama where he suffered defeat by Scipio's army which put an end to all resistance on the part of Carthage at that time.

A few years ago Habib Bourguiba took an old fishing boat from the islands when he fled to Libya to escape from the French. You can see the weatherbeaten boat in an enclosure at Kraten Headland, also the small house where he took refuge. Opposite the house there is a little museum which has photostat copies of letters which the President wrote while he was in exile seeking aid for his country.

8. Gabes, Medenine, The 'Ksars' and Matmata

Herodotus gave the name 'oasis' to the small fertile parts of an otherwise arid desert. These are caused by water coming to the surface for some reason in the form of shallow pools. Others gush out like springs as at Siwa in the Western desert of Egypt which has some 200 separate sources. Many people in the West envisage an oasis as something like a well in the middle of the desert with a dozen palm trees. Admittedly some are very small but others are big enough to sustain towns as at Gabes and Tozeur while again Siwa is a vast fertile raft 50 miles long by five miles wide completely cut off by a vast sea of sand.

Gabes, at the head of the Gulf of the same name, is watered by a stream – the Oued Gabes. The small town edges the oasis, for such a precious spot cannot afford to give up its richness for housing. It is some 70 miles from Sfax and the Kerkenna Islands. The town is built over the Roman site of Tacape and many of the houses have a quaint appearance due to the fact that sections of broken Roman pillars and dressed stone make up parts of their walls.

Should you drive from Sfax to Gabes in the early winter you may be lucky enough to see camel herding in the stretch of desert between the sea and the road. The terrain is flat and there seems to be a camel behind every sand dune. Slowly each makes its way from one patch of thorny scrub to another. The herdsmen know their animals individually and the beasts, aware of this, munch to their heart's content and then wander on to the next choice morsel knowing that master has reserved it especially for them.

How they get enough sustenance from such meagre fare is puzzling yet they thrive and the fluffy youngsters, still suckled by their mothers, take a nibble now and then and are quite content to frisk around. Considering that a camel usually carries a load for twenty-five miles a day, sometimes going for three days without water, it is a pleasure to see them without harness or saddles just mooching along enjoying themselves. They make a dramatic picture, one as old as time, when they gather in lines behind the cameleer in the evening and walk off into the dusk silhouetted against the fading skyline.

The town of Gabes was badly damaged during the last war when Montgomery and the Free French captured it from the Germans in 1943. Bernard Newman in his book 'North African Journey' written in 1955 records how he met an old French soldier in Gabes who said – 'In MY war – the first – generals used to be well clear of the front and the fighting. But I remember when the English captured Gabes. The Germans and Italians left at 7.30 a.m. – and Montgomery himself was here soon after noon.'

The town has been rebuilt and is rather spread out but large maps on the outskirts like those in Kairouan, are helpful in finding your way around. It is wedged between the river Gabes and the sea, the main hotels being strung along the beach. The oasis is on the far side of the river and for some extraordinary reason also practically edges the sea. Its paths and tracks are narrow for every inch that can be used for cultivation is utilized. So much is growing that the labyrinth of footpaths become confusing and you could easily get lost. Little streams can be crossed by palm tree trunk bridges. Fences are made of palm fronds laced together, and very pretty they look. The palm trees are tall and under them fig and fruit trees grow with vegetables, fruit and flowers in turn growing beneath them. Somehow there is enough water and penetrating sunlight for it all. It is almost impossible to describe this amazing fertility. That great historian, Pliny the Elder, wrote about it in Roman times and it was the same then as we see it today. He recorded in minutest detail the terrible eruption of Vesuvius which destroyed Pompeii and the conquest of Britain by Claudius in

A.D. 119 and brought the same keen observation to bear on Gabes and wrote –

> In the midst of the African sands there is a town called Tacape where the soil is well cultivated and wonderfully fruitful. The town extends in all directions for about 3,000 paces. Here is found a fountain with an abundant supply of water, which is only used at ordained times; here grows a high palm and beneath the palm an olive. and under that a fig tree. Under the fig tree grows a pomegranate, and beneath that again a vine. More-over, beneath these are sown, first corn, then vegetables or grass, each sheltering the other.

The oasis covers four square miles and has some 300,000 date palms. If you are there during the date harvest, as I was, every person you meet, both young and old, has a few slender stalks under an arm weighed down at one end with shiny brown fruit as if hung with chocolates. A date never tastes so delicious as when plucked from its stalk and popped straight into the mouth.

The flight of the Holy Family into Egypt is said to have taken place during the date season and the Virgin Mary to have enjoyed the fruit so much that the mark of her teeth has remained imprinted along date stones ever since.

It would be easier to say what does not grow in this lush green-ness than give a list of what you will see. The colour is vivid for besides the exotic flowers and their reflections in the water, there are the orange, lemon and banana trees. The scent of blossoms is almost overpowering and yet such mundane things as tobacco and henna also thrive in this strange place. The best way to enjoy Gabes is to hire a horse and carriage, or a taxi, through the Syndicat d'Initiative and visit the parts of the oasis which are open and then on to Chenini and a small Roman dam with a pretty cascade. You take the road out of Gabes towards Sfax. Opposite the Agip service station turn left into the oasis signed 'Chenini' and follow a palm-shaded metalled road for three kilometres through the oasis. Chenini is a straggling place overhung with palms through which the square minaret of its little mosque points to the sky. In the village square you will see a signpost with the word 'Cascade'. You follow the metalled road for a further kilometre until you come to a T junction. Turn left and in less than a kilometre you come to a clearing where, damned by some Roman masonry, there is a shady pool. A cascade tumbles into the water. There are always people sitting here or talking quietly while children play and run, for to the Arab the sound of water is like music.

If from Gabes you turn south east along G.P. 1, the main road to Medenine, you will come to Mareth in some 12 miles, a small town but of great importance during the last war when it gave its name to the Mareth Line. It was of strategic value because the Oued Zigzaou flowing from the Matmata mountains to the sea acted as a natural line of defence. Although this dried up during the hot season the steep banks formed a tank barrier. Originally it was created to protect the Tunisians should an Italian attack come from Libya. By a quirk of fate it was the Allies who were forced to attack it against the Germans. During the fighting Mareth almost ceased to exist. Happily today the town is rebuilt and tourists visit the Artisanat shop near the local inn without anything to remind them of the recent strife. However, there is an obelisk erected to the memory of the Free French and two German blockhouses to see for those who might wish to recall the final phases in the North African campaign.

Medenine, which has an air-conditioned motel on the outskirts, has grown up on either side of a river, the Oued Smar, and, as so often happens in towns divided by rivers, one side is modern and the other old and established. It has a population of 5,000 and the modern section has up-to-date administrative buildings and a much photographed signpost reading CAIRO 2,606 – probably a left-over of the last war.

The oldest part on the northern bank of the river has a busy open square marketplace but its chief attraction is a collection of strange looking dwellings behind an open archway, surrounding what must have been an old Bedouin caravanserie, known as 'ghorfas'. This is one of the best preserved and most easily visited example, but there are others in the area. They are barrel vaulted structures made of clay, about eight feet high and open at one end. There are no windows and the open end of each ghorfa faces into the square. As the original owner prospered and required more storage space he first added to the row at ground level up to his neighbour and then started a second and third storey on top. This saved ground space and improved the defensive capability for the whole community. The resulting buildings all stuck together resemble a large beehive the upper storeys being reached by primitive stairways, often only of protruding stones.

From Medenine you turn south on G.P. 19 to explore the desert region beyond Foum Tatahouine. On the way you will cross more dried up oueds and may see specimens of the depth gauges used to record flood levels. Some of these are simple marked sticks while others made of concrete have a form of tell-tale device included to record the maximum height reached by the water and enable it to be read off after a flood subsides. It is as well to stress again here that the suddenness with which these dried up river beds can be turned into raging torrents in a bad rainy season. On rare occasions vehicles stuck in the mud of what appeared to be a dried up ford, have been swept away before their occupants could even get out and reach the bank.

From Medenine you turn south on G.P. 19 for 30 miles to Tatahouine which is a nice little town with its new Gazelle hotel and hillside park near the town hall. Besides the usual flower beds and trees some Roman fragments are placed here and there for decoration. The small marketplace itself is park-like edged with arches, earthenware pots and other pieces of Roman masonry, so that it is difficult to reconcile the fact that the town was the site of a camp before the Second World War for French convicts of the 'African Disciplinary Battalions'.

From Tatahouine you can make a tour of the 'Ksars', small fortified hill villages now disused, three of which are close to the town. Although the way to them is more track than road, a good sturdy car or Land Rover makes the journey feasible. The first little village is Beni Barka and there is a sign to it on the left shortly after leaving Tatahouine. It is a barren place with a little tuft of scrub here and there but you can see the ruins of a stone fortress on top of a rocky cliff. Most of the people have moved from the hilltop dwellings and live down on the plain in cave-like enclosures. Several women passed our car while we were driving carrying water pots tied to their foreheads by esparto rope and balanced on their backs.

Also from Tatahouine, some five miles distant on the Remada road, there is a small inn which has converted some nearby 'ghorfas' into 'hotel' rooms for tourists. More sophisticated is the guesthouse at Ksar Haddada. This also had once been 'ghorfas' but the cubbyhole rooms are now fitted with 'mod cons' and there is a good chef.

Chenini, not to be confused with the village of the same name in the Gabes oasis, is the most picturesque of the 'ksars'. It is high on a sugar loaf mountain, the top of which can almost be reached by driving up a series of Swiss type lacets over very rough terrain. The government have built a tiny village on the plain for the people but most of them prefer their eagle nests on the high slopes. The summit is literally a honeycomb of caves whose fronts have been bricked in to make homes. There is a guesthouse made from a large cave divided into rooms. As you climb towards the summit the lunar landscape is reddish in colour and barren, yet there are quite a number of acacia and palm trees. We saw several buzzards perched on cairns which flew off into trees as we approached. As we climbed higher the air became cooler and the sandy plain below seemed like a great lake, cinnamon coloured in the sunlight. The palm trees appeared to be giant green starfish and reminded me of a description given by a Frenchman who said that from a height palm trees resembled nothing so much as green rockets fired into space and suddenly becoming fixed. We stopped our car half way up the mountain on an outcrop of rock and got out. The silence was such that we could hear people talking high above us because the mountain side acted as a sounding board. Then we heard dogs barking. We looked upward at the busy life above and could see minute dots which we took to be goats moving about. Tiny robed

figures walked swiftly along the ledges which were stacked up on top of each other like a pack of cards. How strange that these sure footed hilltop people should be cousins of the troglodytes of Matmata.

Matmata was one particular place I had longed to visit ever since I first arrived in Tunisia, but during my first stay I was disappointed. However, at long last I was to go and my husband decided that if the piste was passable we could drive there over the Matmata mountains from Matameur.

We left Tatahouine after lunch and made our way back to Medenine and took highway G.P. 1 out of the latter for about three miles. We then branched off to the left at Matameur which has larger 'ghorfas' than Medenine many of which are still used. They were just beyond a cemetery and built in the traditional square. The village elders were holding a meeting in the centre but stopped and smiled as we enquired about the way and if there had been any rain locally during the last few days. There had been no rain and the piste was in perfectly good shape so we took our leave with many blessings on our heads for a safe journey. We set off for Matmata about half past three in the afternoon.

We drove along a salt flat type of road across an open sandy plain having to go very slowly now and then to negotiate rough stony patches where dried up oueds had scarred the surface. The way was straight. Ahead of us the rose coloured hills of Matmata jutted into the blue, fissured by centuries of wind and scorching sun. Occasionally there were small plots of cultivation for, although the desert appears empty, there is always a stone dwelling or two and palm trees which mean there is underground water. The Arabs have a saying that 'The palm needs its head in the sun and its feet in water'. A cloud of dust before us gradually grew into a bus which is the only link with the hill villages. The mountains drew nearer and we began to climb. After the long flat drive we now twisted and turned through strange eroded ravines. The road switched back and forth and small villages came and went. Shepherds in long robes kept watch over a few sheep and goats nibbling at scraggy greenish scrub. Soon the lacets got higher and

17   *Pools in the oasis at Gabes*

the plain below sank further and further away. We edged around yet another village clinging to a ledge in a U turn and on the far side a cliff had become so eroded and full of elongated holes that it looked like a Grimms fairy tale castle. The air was cooler, children waved as we went by. We climbed still higher for many of the jebels rise to over 2,000 feet. The roadway narrowed and driving became more difficult. The gravel and sand had been washed away by flooding and had not been repaired. Suddenly the deep valley on my right was suffused with turquoise and pink clouds as if we were flying and from beneath the veils a great silver moon suddenly sailed into view. Sunset appeared over the crags above us on the left and for a few magical moments it was sunset and moonlight together with glowing fantastic colours fading into each other. The sun sank beneath the rim above us, the colours faded and the moon asserted its right in the evening sky.

The narrow lacets worsened, and we had to crawl around curves at a snail's pace. We had been told it was some 40 kilometres to Matmata but our speedometer read far more and we were still climbing. We continued on certain that we should find a sign shortly and start to descend but the road became more serpentine and steeper. Luckily the moon kept complete darkness at bay and the great ledges of stone that we were driving over were shiny as alabaster. We went slower and slower convinced we should puncture the sump. 'What shall we do if we meet someone coming the other way?' I asked Tony. 'We won't meet anyone,' he replied grimly, 'no one would be so foolish as to drive in these mountains in the dark. Keep your eyes open for another signpost.' We had seen a few here and there but they were so weathered that we could not make them out very well. Occasionally we did see one and I climbed out with a torch and as usual could only read the word Matmata – never how many kilometres away. We thought our luck could hold out no longer – it seemed that either we must have a puncture or damage the underside of the car and, if neither of those, we must surely meet someone coming in the opposite direction so we kept an eye open for passing places. The moon climbed higher and it got lighter. Now and then shepherds appeared with a few animals looking like monks with the hoods of their burnouses over their heads against the night air.

At last we began to descend and finally after 70 kilometres we reached Matmata. Looking back I realize that people have very hazy ideas about long distances if they do not travel that way themselves. I do not advise such a trip for others unless it is done in daylight in a very stout car or Land Rover and with an experienced driver. In our case it just so happens that my husband, a Gunner in the British Army, has spent most of his career testing new types of vehicles, loves driving and is used to difficult terrain. He said our drive reminded him of another officer's story during the last war in the Tunisian campaign when travelling with a small detachment. Not sure where he was he asked how far to a certain place and the reply came 'About two gun shots, sir.' He carried on for some distance with his men until he met another local and asked the same question. 'About two gun shots away,' was the same reply. 'Well, chaps,' he said turning to his weary soldiers, 'at least we're holding our own.'

The trouble with us when we reached Matmata is that we could not see it. It is a fact that I have been driven through it but as by the time we got there the moon had waned and it was very dark it was too dangerous to drive around sightseeing because we might have fallen into one of the Matmata dwellings. So reluctantly I must admit I have still not seen Matmata. I must further admit that it was sheer bliss to be back again on a straight, smooth metalled road. We drove swiftly back to Gabes and the Oasis Hotel where we enjoyed an excellent dinner and with our wine toasted the villagers of the Matmata mountains.

Matmata is said to be a place which no traveller should fail to visit! It has a population of 6,000 and is an oasis although it appears to cover a flat plain some 1,340 feet high. From an aircraft the landscape must resemble the moon with its crater-like pits. Yet surely it is more beautiful with its white rounded mosque domes, plots of green studded with palm trees, curving black roadways and the mountain range sheltering it. The extraordinary living quarters, well insulated against searing summer days and freezing cold winter nights, are some 25 feet down into the rock below the surface of the ground and are described in the first chapter. Because of the depth a home can be of two storeys and to add an extra room or two is child's play. All that is needed is to burrow out a little more space through the soft stone. Many dwellings have charming sunken courtyards open to the sky, where fruit trees flourish and give shade, door openings are decorated and stairways are ablaze with pots of flowers. A few of these underground houses have been connected by tunnels and turned into an unusual inn.

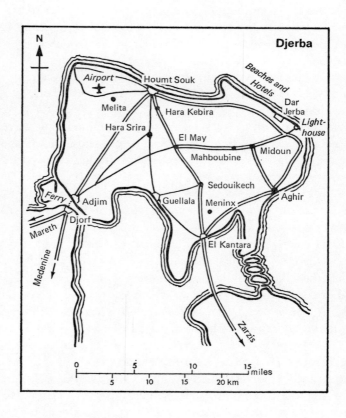

9. Zarzis and the Island of Jerba

Zarzis, some 37 miles from Medenine and in its governorate, is a comparatively new town having come into being during the French occupation. Together with three small villages and some outlying buildings it occupies a coastal oasis of considerable size which has about 500,000 palm trees and 115,000 olive trees irrigated by small canals. The landward side of the oasis is planted with acacias and eucalyptus to prevent soil erosion. Although fruit and vegetables are also grown the production is not large as the artesian wells have a high salt content.

The route to Zarzis is interesting for you drive through miles of olive groves which look as though they have sprung out of dry yellow sand before you reach the town. They are regimented in long lines and come right up to the roadway on either side. It was a stroke of genius on the part of the leading French agriculturists during the 1950s to try this experiment on what was supposed to be arid desert. The scheme included the settling of wandering Accara Bedouin families to tend the plantations, which again was said to be impossible but happily the nomads have taken to this steady occupation and settled down.

The women of Zarzis wear enormous colourful turbans and carry their wares on top of them. They are usually unveiled and effect dangling silver earrings and their arms clink with heavy silver bracelets. Their full, gipsy-like skirts are long and of gaudy material beneath which you get glints of silver anklets. Many of the men have forsaken the small red 'chechia' type of skull cap and wear the 'mudhala' – the wide-brimmed straw hat which is far more sensible to ward off the sun. Everyone seems happy and gregarious. The market stalls and frontless shops are as colourful as the clothes of the people and there is much laughter and bargaining.

Zarzis has become a coastal resort during the last few years with its pleasant climate of warm winters and not excessively hot summers. Hotels nestle in palm groves along the fine sandy coast yet nearly edge into the sea and there are all kinds of beach attractions such as sailing, swimming, water skiing, pedalos, underwater fishing, horse and camel riding. Also it makes a good base for inland excursions or for visiting the island of Jerba.

By car from Zarzis it is 32 miles to Jerba. From Medenine there is a shorter route to the island via the ferry at Djorf, which operates about every 20 minutes from early in the morning until late in the evening. It can take three cars and the crossing lasts from 20 to 30 minutes. You arrive at Adjim and there is a sponge market by the small fishermen's harbour which is always a great draw for tourists.

The other road to Jerba from Zarzis is more fascinating for it eventually comes to El Kantara causeway which is about four miles long. This is built over an old Roman route and cuts right across the sea at ground, or should I say 'water', level so that on a sunny, calm day you are under the illusion that you are driving through silken turquoise water which melts into the sky in the distance with only a thin dark blue line to denote the horizon. Sometimes flocks of flamingoes skim along the surface like a misty pink cloud. Little wonder that Jerba is believed to be Homer's island of the lotus eaters.

Ulysses was said to have set sail homewards with a small fleet after the glory and spoils he had won at Troy. Not content with this he landed on the coast of the fierce Cicons whose town he plundered and held a feast on the booty. They were caught carousing by a fresh force of warriors and just managed to escape on board their ships with the loss of several men. They ran into a storm which tore their sails to tatters and on the tenth day they were fortunate enough to sight an island where they went ashore for fresh water. It was Jerba.

Ulysses sent messengers ahead to see if they would be well received. The island people were indeed lotus eaters, living on a plant named lotus which so dazed their senses that they cared for nothing but dreamy idleness in the languid air of the island, where everything was beautiful and did not change. Even the fruit could be had by stretching out the hand and plucking it from the trees. Once strangers had tasted the flowery food, offered by the gentle islanders they did not have the desire to leave but wished to remain for ever. Tennyson has told of the fate that awaited lotus eaters –

Branches they bore of that enchanted stem.
Laden with flower and fruit, whereof they gave
To each, but who so did receive of them,
And taste, to him the gushing of the wave
Far, far away did seem to mourn and rave
On alien shores; and if his fellow spake,
His voice was thin, as voices from the grave;
And deep-asleep he seem'd, yet all awake,
And music in his ears his beating heart did make.
They sat them down upon the yellow sand,
Between the sun and moon upon the shore;
And sweet it was to dream of Fatherland,
Of child, and wife, and slave; but evermore
Most weary seemed the sea, weary the oar,
Weary the wandering fields of barren foam.
Then someone said, 'We will return no more';
And all at once they sang. 'Our island home
Is far beyond the wave; we will no longer roam.'

When Ulysses saw what a spell the lotus had worked on his messengers he had them dragged back by force, tied to benches on the ships, while the rest of his men he hurried on board before they could eat the flower and fall under the spell of inglorious ease. Toiling at their oars, they left the magic island. So Ulysses and his men crossed the sea to fall upon perils of another land inhabited by the Cyclopes.

Jerba retains another connection with antiquity – the little town of Meninx. This was because of a small shell fish called the murex. It secretes colourless liquid in a gland which when exposed to the air turns a deep purple. This was the most prized dye of ancient times and was known to be a 'fast' colour. Jerba was one of the sources of this dye which was known as 'Tyrian Purple' since it originated in Tyre and Sidon. Indeed the Sidonians were able to produce a variety of shades from the purple such as crimson, violet, rose and heliotrope. The Ptolemies had their sails bordered with purple. Cleopatra's sails at Actium were purple. It became part of the trappings of royalty and nobility and was reserved exclusively for the aristocracy. Unfortunately, like any other decaying fish, the vast mounds of murex shells gave off a fearful stench and so, to use modern terminology, the status symbol was bought at the price of pollution. Murex shell fish can still be found on the beaches in the southern part of the island.

Before you reach the causeway crossing to Jerba there is a pleasant drive from Zarzis through olive groves once more like those leading into the town and tended in the same way. Shortly after the village of Sidi Chemmakh on Highway 117 you come to the causeway that leads to the island.

If you wish to go to Jerba by air nothing could be simpler as there are both direct flights from Europe, mostly charter, or you can fly Tunis Air from Heathrow (or Caledonian from Gatwick) to Tunis with onward connecting flights. Flying time to Tunis is about $2\frac{1}{2}$ hours and times on to Jerba about another 40 minutes.

Jerba, the largest of the North African Islands, some 17 miles long by 14 wide, is separated from the mainland by the Gulf of Bou Grara which varies in depth from 20 to 80 feet. Most of the inhabitants are Berbers and speak an ancient dialect. They are a gentle, slow moving people with a friendly desire to please and are often referred to in Tunisia as 'grocers'. Jerbans are renowned for going to the mainland, opening small grocery shops and working hard. When they make a modest fortune they return home to enjoy it. A typical story goes that a teenage farm labourer went to the mainland to become rich. After working hard for twenty years he accumulated enough money to retire and was asked if he would do so in Tunis. 'No!' he replied, 'I want to enjoy my old age and lead a restful life. I shall return to Jerba and buy a farm.'

The island, surrounded by white sandy beaches, seems like one continuous oasis and the fruits are famous – apples, peaches, figs, pears, apricots, dates, lemons, mandarines, grenadines and oranges – only the lotus fruit is missing! Centuries of invasion have caused the people to leave the coast and move inland where every inch is cultivated. Water is very scarce, much of it having to be drawn from ancient artesian wells. Being on the same latitude as Los Angeles, Bermuda and Madeira, Jerba has a warmer climate than the resorts in the north. In summer the temperature can soar to 100 degrees Fahrenheit but there is always a light breeze from the sea. Even when I was there in November the thermometer was on the 70s and the swimming delightful. In midwinter it is usually above 60° so that you can swim practically right through the year.

Nearly two million palm and 60,000 olive trees thrive on the island together with vegetables and the other fruit. There are over a dozen hotels spread out, well away from each other, edging the north eastern shore. One of the longest established ones, extremely well run and in Moorish style, is suitably named The Ulysses Palace. It has 130 rooms, swimming pool, lounges, a boutique, hair dressing, mini golf, night club and all kinds of water sports. Another one, The Hotel Les Sirenes where we stayed, has the same sort of facilities. Its outdoor swimming pool is filled from a natural spring which produces water the colour of brown Windsor soup due to its iron content but maintains the temperature well into the eighties. One night before dinner I lowered myself into it gingerly. It was delightfully warm but it was strange to swim with a few other people and just see heads seemingly without bodies bobbing up here and there. When I returned to my room and rinsed my bathing suit the water turned brown but that was as nothing compared to my bath water. However I felt invigorated so perhaps thermal water, as used by the ancient Romans, is beneficial.

Whichever hotel you stay in you can of course visit the others for a change of scene. Most of them arrange special programmes on certain nights such as folklore cabarets, barbecues or tennis tournaments so it is well worth enquiring what is on.

As if to anticipate such a life for visitors there is now the vast Dar Jerba built alongside a three-quarter mile length of white sandy beach, a complete tourist village with some 2,500 beds. It consists of four hotels, each named after local flowers : Jasmin, Narjiss, Dahlia and Zahra and accommodation is split into four categories : super luxury, luxury, semi luxury and standard. But these are no ordinary hotels, for each has been designed in the local style of architecture with much use of domes and cupolas, graceful arches and slender pillars. The majority of the rooms are on the ground floor with gardens and palms everywhere and the beach is never more than a couple of minutes' walk away. At the top end of the scale, there is the super de luxe : miniature air-conditioned maisonette, with a sitting-room and bathroom on the ground floor and a twin-bedded room with balcony on the upper one, refrigerator, television and room service. Next is the de luxe with its own shaded patio, spacious bedroom, bathroom and high arched roof in traditional Jerban style, air-conditioning and room service. The third grade is the semi de luxe again with a patio, twin bedded room and bathroom, air-conditioning and room service. The fourth category is standard, with smaller patio, twin beds and private shower but no room service.

There is a Children's Hotel, which has 20 rooms (80 beds), restaurant, play areas, its own three bay swimming pool and marionette theatre. Here youngsters can spend the day or stay the complete holiday, swim, eat and sleep under the supervision of trained personnel.

The 'tourist village' has a central area with a de luxe restaurant (each hotel also has its own), a night club, discotheque, an open air cinema that seats 500 people, a casino and four swimming pools which are heated during the winter, a coffee shop, a restaurant which serves Tunisian food and several bars. There is a souk offering a wide selection of items, a post office, bank, travel agency, car hire office and ample parking space.

Dar Jerba has its own radio station with piped music to every room, three channels to choose from and regular news bulletins at various times of the day, one of the languages being English.

There are water skiing, skin diving and a sailing school with 50 small yachts. For inland-based sportsmen, there is tennis, volley ball, horse and camel riding.

The Danish architect, Claus Bremer, has shown good taste and imagination in planning this spacious holiday world which combines Tunisian style with European comfort. President Bourguiba officially opened Dar Jerba in 1973. There are guided tours about the island and cars to be hired and as Jerba is flat it is an ideal place to hire a bicycle to go about leisurely. The speed limit is thirty miles an hour but distances are short and everything so enchanting that one would not wish to go more quickly.

To get to Houmt Souk, the capital, from the area of the hotels at Sidi Mahrez and La Seguia beaches, you drive north-west along the coastal road. Beyond this where there is a shelving beach there are usually women washing wool in the sea. They paddle into the water, fully clothed, up to their knees and then rinse the wool over and over again in a flat loosely woven basket until it is soft and white. Who says that salt water is bad for wool?

You soon see the little fortress on the seashore which guards Houmt Souk. It is known as the Borj el Kebir – the Large Tower – and was built in 1284, later enlarged by the Spaniards and then by the Corsair Dragut in 1567. Dragut had no sympathy for the Spaniards and when he captured their fort he had them all beheaded. Not content with this he ordered the skulls to be made into a pyramid which stayed as a grim reminder near the port for some 400 years. During the nineteenth century a humane Bey issued a command to have them buried. A bronze plaque marks the spot today.

Houmt Souk itself is a bright, tidy little town its quiet harbour lying in the shadows of the Borj el Kebir. In the marketplace, robed Jerbans sit under the plane trees surrounded by mounds of rugs and vegetables, goats, chickens and rows of earthenware amphorae, the classical jars for wine or water. The shadowy souks are close by with their covered stalls and frontless shops where you can haggle over the price of rugs, blankets, horse and camel saddles or brass and copper oddments. The best buy however is silver and gold jewellery, ancient and modern, for both are sold by weight, not workmanship, and many pieces are beautifully designed. The artisanat shop has special Jerban wares as well as those from the rest of the country and its telephone number is easy to remember – Houmt Souk 40.

Jerban architecture is charming and everything is on a small scale. Little rounded domes are known as 'menzels' and most houses have one. Walls are thick and culminate in domed ceilings so that, outside, the houses look like snow-white sparkling igloos. Square towers are often added to dwellings, especially the farm houses and due to their elevated position with open apertures they give ventilation. These buildings in turn have high walls, concealing open courtyards set with plants and trees, and these are as sparkling white as the menzels. As on the mainland any embellishment such as wrought iron work is painted bright sky blue.

The two villages of Hara Kebira and Hara Srira look no different from any other mud-walled Jerban village save that some of the white walls are decorated with seven branched candlesticks and rough drawings of fish. The men wear the same clothes as in other places and the women wear sifsaris and many are veiled. Yet their inhabitants are Jews, descendants of refugees from Jerusalem after the city was sacked in A.D. 70. They are probably the oldest and purest Jewish communities in Africa, and their synagogue is a centre of pilgrimage 33 days after Passover every year. It is built over the site of previous synagogues and has a modern hospice for pilgrims facing it. The original building dates from 600 years before Christ.

You enter to be greeted by the wailing chants of elders reading the Thora. In an adjoining chamber the rabbi, who from his dress might have stepped out of the Old Testament, presents you with a headcloth and opens two panelled doors to reveal parchment scrolls of the Thora encased in silver cylinders.

As we had gone back so far in time it seemed appropriate to visit Meninx, the ancient Roman capital. The remains of a temple and mosaic fragments have been found and perhaps a robe of 'Royal Purple' will be unearthed one day!

Talking of dress is a reminder of the colourful costumes worn by Jerban brides. Young Tunisians these days tend to marry in the European fashion but in some regions, particularly Jerba, marriage customs have been preserved. When the big day arrives the bride, clad in lavishly embroidered robes, sits on a throne of flowers attended by her maids-in-waiting while the male members of the tribe play musical instruments accompanied by women who sing joyous songs. Everyone is gay despite the fact that the last few days have been spent in celebrations. Then the bride holds up her hands to her chief maid-in-waiting who anoints the palms with an ointment mixed with henna as a sign of purification. Next the bride is wrapped in a burnous and the hood put over her head to protect her from evil spirits. She is led from her parents' house, lifted up and placed in a palanquin on a camel's back. The palanquin is hung with multicoloured rugs and the camel's harness is decorated with woollen tassels. Then comes the olive tree ceremony when the camel is led through an olive grove followed by the wedding guests. This is a rite symbolising fertility and the breaking away from parents. It is reminiscent of the clause in the Christian marriage service when the clergyman says; 'The wife shall be as the fruitful vine upon the walls of thy house. The children like the olive branches round thy table.' The wedding procession continues on its way and follows the bride on her camel through the village to her husband's house.

The 'Stambali' is a Jerban dance performed by men on gay occasions such as weddings. The performers wear wide pantaloons which reach to and are caught just below the knee. These are white and similar to those worn in Egypt beneath the long robes called 'glabias'. White turbans are folded about red chechias and jackets, which are sometimes of embroidered cloth or animal skins sewn with shells or other decoration, reach to the wrist and are gathered in about the waist. Music is provided by wooden clappers. Each man holds a short stick in his right hand and the complicated steps of the dance are repeated over and over again.

The 'Stambali' on some occasions can be used to cast out evil spirits who haunt a person or a dwelling. In the latter case the dancers kneel in the house and rock back and forth. They move faster and faster frantically chanting purifying words. The rocking increases in speed until the dancers are on the verge of collapse and in a fainting state. It is said that the evil spirit seldom returns!

Each Jerban village seems to specialize in something. The people in a small place called Fatou a few miles from Houmt Souk make woven rush mats. All the villagers join in this trade the ages varying from 17 to 70 years. At Sedouikech they make camel muzzles, fishing nets, baskets and the conical straw hats that many Jerban women wear at a jaunty angle often on top of their sifsaris. The Jewish communities are known for their intricate silver jewellery. In Guellala and Fahmine it is pottery.

In Guellala the many curious hillocks you see are primitive kilns on which pottery debris has accumulated through the years. To watch the potters at work is always fascinating. In Guellala not only do the men seem to enjoy onlookers but they sometimes offer you some clay to 'throw' and try your hand at making an oddment, say a small vase, of your own.

Local material is used and colours range from yellow to red. Ordinary clay is left to soak one or two days in hollows dug into the ground and filled with sea water, which bleaches it. The artisan then kneads the clay with his feet to make a malleable fine paste to use. Now the creative work begins. The potter's wheel consists of two wooden discs, the lower one, operated by foot, turns the upper disc to which it is connected and the potter throws the clay on the top one and moulds his wares with ease. From time to time he moistens his fingers in a small trench filled with liquid mud. The vessels he makes are dried in a cool place before being fired.

Weaving and rug making are also fascinating to watch. Wool is supplied in part by local livestock (a camel is shorn once a year) and there are 1,200 to 1,500 tiny workshops in the island mostly in houses so that weaving has become a cottage industry. The women who wash the wool in the sea draw it out then dry and comb it before spinning it on their olive wood spindles. It is then ready for dyeing which is also done in the island.

Some seven miles from Guellala there is yet another little town with tiny menzels and baby towers, still in the same pure white with blue doors and balconies, not to mention at least ten mosques. This is Adjim where the sponge fishermen live. The boats go out at dawn, their lateen sails unfurled and skim along the smooth water to the sponge fishing grounds. The sails are pulled down and the search begins. Glass bottomed pails are immersed in the sea to enable the sea bed to be inspected. Experienced eyes can spot a sponge through seaweed like a miner spotting gold. Then with a long handled trident, like Neptune himself, the fisherman strikes through the water with a quick movement, stabs the sponge and uproots it. In deeper water men dive down into the depths armed with short handled spears and bring them up festooned with sponges. Some divers use stones as weights to drop to depths of some 70 feet in order to get the best sponges. These do not look like the ones we are used to seeing as in the raw state most are like glutinous, blackish balls of different sizes.

The island is so short of fresh water that, to deal with the influx of tourism, it has been found necessary to pipe it from the mainland. The two traditional sources still much in evidence are wells and collecting cisterns. Typical Jerban wells can be seen everywhere though many today are dried up and disused. The two upright arms of stone covered with plaster and whitewash are raised skyward joined by one or more wooden cross bars forming the drums on which the rope is wound.

In other places you will see large rectangular concrete slabs sometimes 40 or more feet long, sloping towards the centre, where there is a hole to lead the collected valuable rain water into the cistern below.

El May is quite a large village in the centre of the island and its fortified Kharedjite mosque is well known. It reminded me of the fortified 'round' churches on Bornholm, one of the Danish islands, in that it has no windows and is reinforced with flying buttresses.

The island has a fine little museum just on the left of the road leaving Houmt Souk (the name is appropriate and means market centre) which has local ceremonial garments including those for marriage and circumcision. The marriage 'Hope Chest' is a beautiful leather trunk with nail studded decorations. The jewellery is unusual and there are some ancient manuscripts. You can see the various stages of pottery making dating back to Phoenician days which is interesting if you do not have the time to see the real things at Guellala. Opening hours differ in summer and winter. In summer it is from 9.00 – 12.00, 15.00 – 18.00. In winter it is from 9.00 – 12.00, 14.00 – 17.00.

The actual shopping times in Houmt Souk and most of the other villages are from nine o'clock in the mornings until noon and from four o'clock in the afternoons until seven o'clock in the evenings.

While in Jerba I heard of its 'fifth season' during the year and only recently discovered what it meant. It is from a famous quotation about the island by Grevin which runs something like this –

At Sfax the winter will have gone, at Gabes you will find the spring, at Tozeur the summer and at Jerba you will discover the fifth season . . . the fifth season, that climate peculiar to Jerba's summer, so strange, a blend of extreme dryness, seabreeze, night coolness and dew, of something rational and temperate in all things.

Perhaps Ulysses was right to leave the land of the lotus eaters for certainly it almost compels one to stay.

18 Wares in Houmt Souk, Jerba

10. Gafsa and the Jerid Oases

Gafsa, some 225 miles from Tunis, is the first oasis on the road to the south. After the white and blue houses, so typical of most of Tunisia it comes as a surprise to find the buildings in Gafsa not white washed but rose washed. Even the kasbah and the law courts are a deep pinkish colour which is most attractive. It is heartening to think that this small fortress built by the Hafsites in 1434 managed to ward off Dragut in 1551 although it fell some five years later. It changed hands three times during the last world war but fortunately suffered little. Apparently the kasbah was slightly damaged but it is impossible to say which section for it has been skilfully repaired. There are also thermal springs but with a difference. They are not used as such today but remain just as the Romans built them, the water bubbling up into large cisterns, two with shallow steps leading into them and the Roman inscriptions still visible.

However brief your stay these baths are a must because they are just at the bottom of the main street and have a picturesque setting. The largest is in the shade of three tall palm trees which youngsters climb up and pester you to throw coins into the water so that they can dive for them. Do not worry about the boys catching cold on a windy day because the water is about 30° Centigrade. The smallest pool is partly covered by the stone arches of the local Beylical palace and, to add to this stage-like setting, the square minaret of the Great Mosque towers over the scene with its octagonal drum. The minaret is a favourite place for photographers. Its hundred or so steps can be taken in easy stages as they are in

19   A camel working a well on Jerba

short flights and the many arched openings give wonderful panoramas of the town and the emerald green oasis beyond.

Gafsa has some 50,000 inhabitants and is a garrison town. Its great pink Byzantine fort again looks like a stage set and you expect to see Beau Geste striding out at any moment. The Artisanat Centre, near the Kasbah, specializes in gaily coloured carpets of geometrical design. Here you can watch the girls working on their looms. We stayed at the Jugurtha Palace, a 78-room hotel with a delightful swimming pool surrounded by palm trees. It is about four miles from the town at the foot of a pink jebel (hill). Perhaps Gafsa took its pink colouring from the rose coloured jebels which encircle it. These are similar to those which make such a wonderful backdrop in Akaba in Jordan.

Some five miles from Gafsa Lalla Oasis comes into view. 'Lala' means a 'Holy Woman' in the same way as 'Marabout' means a 'Holy Man'. The shrine of a holy man is also called 'Marabout'. You can drive around the oasis or hire a horse and carriage which enables you to visit the narrow earth tracks which are raised above the irrigation canals. As at Gabes there are layers of cultivation under the palm trees which do not produce a good quality date and the wealth of the oasis lies in its other fruits. In the evening it is a pleasant sight to see the camels going down to have their fill of water at the Oued Baiech, the river which borders the oasis.

You leave Gafsa for Tozeur and Nefta by travelling south west. The highway stretches in a straight line as far as the eye can see with pink hills to the right and, between them and the roadway, great clumps of camel scrub grow which, in November, produce tiny red flowers. The small town of Metlaoui-Gare is interesting in that it owes its name to Philippe Thomas, a French veterinary surgeon who discovered the rich deposits of phosphates in the district. The town is now headquarters for the nationalised 'Compagnie des Phosphates de Gafsa'. If you have time you can turn right and call at the main office and ask for a key to the little local museum which gives you an idea of the geological and botanical discoveries in the area. The gardens surrounding the buildings have a few animals. Oddly enough when Philippe Thomas first came to the district it was to study the diseases of goats!

Back on the main road some three miles further on there is another diversion if you wish. You turn right for the Seldja Gorges. You can drive part of the way and then must go on foot if you want to explore further. By following the Oued Seldja upstream you come to a narrow passage not unlike a small edition of Petra's siq known appropriately as 'Sword Thrust'. Beyond this there are more rocky gorges and the phosphate company's light railway.

Back on G.P.3 you continue south west to Tozeur. Finally you come to the first of Tozeur's oases where, it is said that the water was cold as ice until a Marabout spat into it when it miraculously turned therapeutic and warm. More palm trees in straggling lines mark Tozeur itself which obtains its water from some 200 springs forming a river. The oasis, second only to Gabes in size, stretches east and south of the town some 25,000 acres in extent. As at Gafsa the water is 30° Centigrade and the flow is controlled by sluices – a scheme contrived during the thirteenth century. The springs are cleaned out every spring and it is an occasion for celebration with singing and dancing as someone remarked – 'This is a real spring cleaning!'

Seeing Tunisia's incomparable lush oases rimmed with arid desert for the first time is a unique experience and now that Tozeur is to have a new international airport it will open up this part of the country more readily for visitors. The new deep sea port at Gabes will do the same thing for those on cruising holidays.

Tozeur is not as romantic as Gafsa but its architecture is most unusual. The façades of buildings are decorated with yellow bricks laid 'in relief' and these form stylized geometric patterns. The main street, Avenue Bourguiba, is very colourful with open air cafés and frontless shops whose walls are festooned with rugs, kaftans, straw hats and baskets.

The colours are further emphasized by the local women wearing black sifsaris with white borders. There is an Information Office and a shop called 'The Handicraft Centre of the Jerid and Marvels of the Sahara' owned by a local man named Amar Ben

Taleb Sessi. He is an amusing character and if asked will produce a portfolio of press-cuttings about people being delighted with his wares, silver jewellery, saddles, kaftans, rugs and so on. He also claims that he is a poet. Amar writes in the classical Arabic of the Koran, which is very different from the everyday variety and each year he composes a special poem for the President.

Another well-known local character is also called Amar and he has an amazing garden called 'The Paradise' about two miles out of Tozeur, which incidentally is the capital of the Jerid. He is always pleased to see visitors and is proud of the fact that he cuts his roses in March, picks his plums in June, grapes in July and strawberries in February! All this in a lush garden on the very edge of the desert. Sand is kept at arm's length by palm frond fencing and at the other extreme, the entrance to 'Paradise' has a jujube tree of incredible age planted years ago by a holy man, Sidi Bou Ali, whose Marabout stands nearby. You may sample and buy some of Amar's distillations and syrups. The violet syrup tastes like the fondant centres you get in homemade chocolates.

A signpost reading 'M. Tijani's Snake Farm' indicates a third port of call. Mr. Tijani handles snakes and scorpions. He says that vipers can cure cancer and rheumatism but I have not met anyone who can substantiate this claim. He patiently explains that snake venom need not necessarily be dangerous, just on the odd occasion fatal!

Behind the Esso station in Tozeur stands the Zawia of Sidi Mouldi its walls made of the same distinctive yellow brickwork in patterns. This was rebuilt in 1944 and its four-cupola minaret overlooks the town. The arcaded forecourt leads to a madrasah, a religious school whose chambers edge the inner courtyard. Opposite the mosque there is an ornamental arch.

From Tozeur to Nefta, some 15 miles distant, the black asphalt road leads in a straight line through undulating desert. To the left what at first might be thought to be snow in a northern country is in reality the salt crust of a bitter lake.

You reach Nefta through an avenue of eucalyptus trees and at a crossroads a sign indicates the well-known Sahara Palace Hotel.

The Italian architect has planned it in the grand manner and it is on a plateau overlooking the 'Corbeille', the name of the lovely Nefta oasis. Its walls and balconies are patterned in yellow Tozeur brick and it is fully air-conditioned with 100 twin-bedded rooms and 14 apartments. All rooms are equipped with bath and shower, telephone, radio and have balconies with a splendid view of the oasis, the village and the desert. Amenities include a hairdressing salon, boutique, exchange office, reading rooms, tea room, three bars, Moorish cafe, an olympic size swimming pool, a cinema, horse and camel riding, table tennis, tennis and mini golf. Safari expeditions can be arranged and a mini jeep is available for sightseeing.

The Sahara Palace is said to be Brigitte Bardot's favourite hotel, certainly film people use it and during 1973 many of the cast of 'The Little Prince' lived there while making the film.

The Little Prince, with music by Lerner and Loewe brings Saint Exupery's famous tale to the screen. In France both children and grown-ups know it as well as La Fontaine's fables. A film unit of over 100 stayed in Tozeur and Nefta where the desert and oasis areas provided a perfect setting.

The story is about a pilot making a forced landing in the desert where he is found by the little Prince who has come from another planet and tells the pilot about his life there. Also how he has made friends with a fox since he had arrived on earth. On his own planet he had fallen in love with the only rose there. She told him she was the only one of her kind. Yet, the little Prince said, 'I've found many roses on earth – but the fox explained how my rose was quite different because of my love for her. It is only with the heart that you see rightly; essential things are invisible to the eye.' When the pilot had nearly finished mending his aeroplane the little Prince told him, 'The stars are beautiful because one of them contains my flower which cannot be seen here. The desert is beautiful because somewhere it hides a well.' The pilot replies, 'When I was a boy I lived in a house where there was supposed to be buried treasure. No one had ever known how to find it; perhaps no one had ever even looked for it. But it cast an enchantment over the house. Houses, stars and desert – what gives them their beauty is something that is invisible. The fox is right.'

The Sahara Palace Hotel acted as a background for an amusing joke played on some visiting film and stage stars when they were on a golfing holiday. They had been flown down to the south to see the 'Corbeille' and the hotel arranged a desert feast for them. It was a lunch time affair and the guests were to sit cross-legged in a tent in true Bedouin fashion and be served lamb which had been roasted on spits. Two members of the press who were in the party decided to dress up as veiled nobles from a neighbouring kingdom and arranged for a small tent to be set up next to the party one. They let it be known that they would like to have the visiting stars presented to them. Among the distinguished guests were Sean Connery, Stanley Baker, Graham Hill, Michael Medwin, Eric Sykes and Ronnie Carroll. Jeffrey Rayner, who was acting host, led the party to the dignitaries and showed them how to give the greeting 'Salaam'. They were received with great courtesy and it was only when the last guest had filed past that the 'Sheiks' revealed who they were. It was quite an hilarious occasion and no one was more astonished than Jeffrey who is one of Tunisia's most avid admirers and extremely knowledgeable about the country, not to mention knowing many important Arab personages! The guests however took a leaf out of the press members' book. When they all returned to Tunis and attended a reception just before they went home the actors dressed up as visiting nobles and played the part to the manner born – but without speaking. When they unveiled themselves their Tunisian hosts were as amused as they themselves had been at the Sahara Palace Hotel. The disguises were talked about for some time and the story got back to England and was reported in the British national press.

But to get back to the oases country in the south. Perhaps the best view from the Sahara Palace Hotel of the 'Corbeille' is from a tennis court at the edge of the plateau. From here you can look down into the lush oasis which at sunset or in moonlight is as beautiful as even the little Prince would wish. A hundred and fifty bubbling warm springs water some 300,000 palm trees including

70,000 which yield the delicious 'Deglas' dates, the best in the country. The oasis is considered a holy place with many shrines and you can glimpse their white domes through the emerald green of the trees and sometimes see their reflections in the water.

Close to the oasis by a waterfall there is a café where visitors stop to have mint tea or a cooling drink before setting off on a donkey, camel or foot to explore the oasis. You can wander by little streams with vines, mimosas, pomegranates, lemons and other trees beneath the palms. It is wise to hire a guide to show you the oasis and you can get one from your hotel or the Syndicat d'Initiative. Donkeys are a favourite way of getting around and your guide can take you to visit a home or two where women weave or men make pottery. The sifsaris in Nefta are a deep purple colour and some women wear the same black ones with white borders which are seen in Tozeur. In the old quarter of the town there is a sixteenth-century Great Mosque.

The Chott el Jerid which edges Nefta and Tozeur is an enormous saline depression in the northern wastes of the Sahara. It can be crossed much of the year but it is not advisable during the rainy season and should only be done in a party with experienced drivers. The desert is an enigmatical strange place with mirages which constantly change the landscape. Its vast expanses of lonely sand make dawns and sunsets unbelievably lovely and, because of the unexpected and unforeseen things that happen there, it has always appealed to adventurers like Lawrence and Thesiger. However these days safaris are arranged that can take the most timid of tourists into its loneliness for a few days with efficient guides, meals at the correct times, reasonably comfortable rest houses and bring them back in time to catch the return flight home.

The genuine properly equipped tourist bent on adventure will come to no harm in the ordinary way. The cause of trouble and often tragedy is the type of person who thinks he can adopt the Arab's fatalistic attitude of 'En sha Allah' – 'it is the will of God' and rush into the desert leaving everything to chance. He lacks the matching Arab hereditary skills which enable him to survive in the harsh environment. He does not recognize the signs of an impending sandstorm or the difference between firm and shifting sands and with little knowledge of navigation or mechanical skill tends to just 'take off'. Worst of all he does not tell anybody his plans so that he cannot be found if he does not return on time and this causes anxiety to all concerned.

The story is told of two youths who, complete with cameras, vanished behind the sand-dunes where they thought unknown dangers awaited them and would make a good article called 'Thrills and Spills in the Desert'. Organized safaris along known routes did not appeal and they decided to get off the beaten track and explore further. They soon got stuck in the sand but were fortunate to be seen by some Arabs who helped them get back on the track. A few hours later they decided it was time to get off the trail again and made towards what appeared to be a clump of trees in the distance. Again they foundered in a sea of sand and could not make any progress. What they had taken to be a clump of trees turned out fortunately to be four Arabs on camels coming towards them. Again they were helped back on to firm ground with much sweating and heaving. The cameleers went on their way one saying to the other, 'These men are like children for they do not know the difference between hard and soft sand.'

The third attempt to go off into the desert wastes luckily finished the expedition. Having managed to get some miles off the real track they made for some mounds of boulders hoping to find harder ground. The ground was so hard in fact that they bounced on to a boulder and were in the odd situation of being in the air and all the wheels off the ground! Again some camel herders appeared as from nowhere and helped them get their vehicle dislodged. This proved to be enough to convince them and it was decided to go back to base and leave the magic of the desert to others. One disappointed youth said to the other, 'Whoever produced this myth about being alone in the desert wastes obviously never saw the recent T.V. commercial on a well-known brand of cigarette. There seems to be an Arab behind every sand-dune.' In reality they had been extremely lucky for the desert can be a very lonely, hostile place.

Edging the Chott el Jerid are a number of small oases of which it is claimed that Mansouah is the prettiest. Kebili is held to be the most important and there are excursions to it and on to Douz, some 18 miles beyond. You can stay in either place overnight at small inns quite cheaply. Beyond these oases the real desert starts.

Kebili was a stop on the slave trade route and, save for a few fragments of Roman columns, it looks just what it is, a stopping off place on the way across the Jerid or a base from which to go further into the desert. Perhaps the people are the major interest here. Many of them migrate during the winter months into the Sahara when the heat is less intense and the grazing better. They are dark skinned often with red hair due to using henna as a dye.

Occasionally you will see members of the Tuareg tribes who are regarded as the purest of the Berber stock. They are descendants of those Berbers who were driven into the desert by the Arab invasion of North Africa in the eleventh century. The men's hair is long, black and silky, the eyes brown or sometimes blue, the noses small and the hands delicate. They are a tall people and wear a head covering, the 'Litham', a type of turban the end of which is drawn over the face so that nothing is seen save the eyes and tip of the nose. The 'Litham' of the nobles is blue, others of the tribe wear white. They are worn to protect the throat and lungs from the sand and are seldom removed which is the reason why the Arabs call them 'People of the Veil.'

The Tuareg nobles do no work but live in the saddle. When a chief dies he is not succeeded by his son but, with the approval of the tribesmen, the eldest son of his eldest sister becomes chief. Today they have fallen largely under the influence of Arab customs and adopted the religion of Islam. Their mosques are usually stone enclosures with a small niche at one end facing Mecca. However they do have several desert 'Monasteries', large tents arranged in a circle. Here the Marabout lives surrounded by believers. These monasteries move when the requirements of the tribes and the need for fresh pastures make it necessary.

Douz resembles a little frontier town with white dwellings and

again is inhabited by nomads. There are always great celebrations
before departing into the desert and the ceremony is sometimes
enacted for visitors. Thursday is market day when camels are
bought and sold. As more and more tourists venture forth to see
the oases, so it is planned to extend the existing routes to the
Leclerc monument and perhaps beyond. This monument recalls
General Leclerc's epic march from Lake Chad in World War II
and is some 55 miles south-west of Medenine. At present it is only
approachable from that direction. A story is told of an incident
during the march when the R.A.F. dropped supplies to the general
and his men. He sent a simple message, 'Merci R.A.F.' The leading
pilot replied, 'Vive le Sport.'

Of the oases near the Algerian frontier Chebika was the one
that appealed to us for some reason. Tony and I decided to drive
there as, although there is only a track to it, this is clearly marked
in maps and there had been no recent rain. We set off from
Tozeur on G.P. 3 for El Hamma and, after some confusion over
which of two equally rough tracks to follow, found the town and
launched ourselves on the road leading some 35 miles north-west
to Chebika. It may be described as G.P. 16 on the map but we had
our doubts about it in several places.

It was a bright, sunny morning and the road stretched straight
ahead with expanses of shallow sandsweeps blown over it here and
there and for the first few miles the going was easy. We were driving along the flattened bottom of an oued which had been dried
up for many years. The road had been laid along this way because,
far away in the mountains, the course of the river that fed it long
ago had been diverted elsewhere.

Further on the road dips slightly and at one place we had to
negotiate quite a high bank of sand but managed to charge over
it at speed. On both sides of the track the desert reached to the
horizon, behind us low lying El Hamma had disappeared and
ahead the tops of the mountains shimmered in a pink heat haze so
that you could not be sure whether they were real or a mirage.
It is a fascinating situation for people who are used to crowded
cities and well worth experiencing. Tufts of camel scrub grew

everywhere presumably kept alive by the dew at night. Gazelles, charming little animals, exist here also and the dew supplies their only liquid. Indeed pet gazelles have to be given very little water in captivity or they will die. Unfortunately we did not see any in Tunisia during this visit but I have seen them in the Western Desert in Egypt and they were so tiny and beautiful that they might have sprung from the little Prince's imagination. Their purplish, shiny hooves are about as large as a thumb nail.

As we drove on we saw what appeared to be low rose coloured clouds on the horizon. Gradually the colour grew into a line of pink hills at the base of which we should find Chebika. The road flattened out again, then rose and fell several times and we had to avoid deep sand drifts by going off to one side. The nearing hills got lighter in colour as we approached. Finally Chebika came into view, a collection of houses behind a white square building and the Marabout of Sidi Sultan. The little mosque is on the edge of a ravine and forms the boundary on one side. There is one shop and a school. Beyond the village lay the precious oasis and we managed to drive around its outskirts without too much difficulty. Frond fences stop the earth tumbling into runnels of water and these have to be cleaned constantly to allow a free flow otherwise the peas, beans and peppers will not survive on the tiny banks. There was the heady scent of flowers with the more pungent smell of mint. Frogs jumped into the water at our approach.

During the blistering heat of summer, water is distributed at night. Because of the abundance of fruit and vegetables, the oasis needs continual attention. Men clear the canals and rivulets with a type of hoe that has been used for centuries, wielding it by hand with one foot in the water and the other on dry land or standing astride the narrow runnels and banking up the rich mud on either side. Above Chebika a waterfall, overhung with palm trees, tumbles down a bare pink ravine, a cooling sound during the heat of the day.

Reluctantly we could only spend a brief time at Chebika before starting back to Tozeur. During our drive in the morning we had noticed in many places flashing reflections of sunlight from the ground and had decided that, on the way back, we should find out what it was. The route was now familiar and we stopped several times to watch camel herding and to inspect our glittering 'crystal'. It seems to be a form of mica and we collected some to bring home as in its way it is as pretty as rough amethyst but with a pearly finish instead of a mauve colouring.

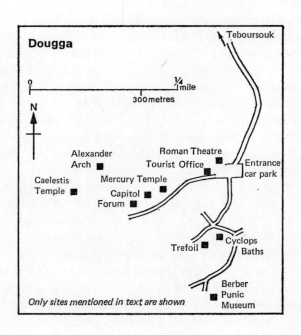

11. The Central Area

Dougga is some 60 miles south-west of Tunis and driving inland along the G.P. 5 you will pass three war cemeteries. The first is a German one at La Mornaghia which has a lone Panzer tank and many stone crosses. At Massicault there is a Commonwealth cemetery on the right hand side of the road where 1,576 officers and men are buried. The simple graves are divided by a few well tended flower beds and edged with fig and eucalyptus trees. In the background stands the Cross of Sacrifice with a row of cypresses.

Medjez el Bab, a largish market town, on the Medjerda river saw strong opposition from the Free French when the Germans were advancing towards Tunis in November 1942. Near what was known as 'Longstop Hill' by allied troops, is another Commonwealth War Graves Cemetery. It is fenced in by a low wall and just inside the entrance there is a large white plaque with the words 'Their name liveth for evermore'. Cypresses stand like sentinels on either side of a slender cross. Little flower beds are between the graves.

Three years ago when I was in Tunisia I was astonished to be taken by friends into this cemetery for a picnic. Then it struck me what a pleasant idea it was to take the Arab attitude that those who have gone like us to join them on such occasions. Birds were singing and we sat beneath some shady trees. After we had finished I wandered around the gravestones. Before one a small bunch of poppies had been laid with a card on which was written 'For all the boys who gave their lives for us to live in a better world'. It was signed 'Peter'. On another gravestone the inscription read, 'F.

Morley. Coldstream Guards. Age 21. Too dearly loved to be forgotten. Goodnight my son until we meet. Mother'. The next had 'Some corner of a foreign field which is forever England'.

Many tombstones were inscribed with just the words 'Rest in Peace' and those men who died and were unknown had headstones engraved with the words 'A soldier of the 1939-45 War. Known only to God'. A large plaque recorded:

> On this famous battleground of the ancient world two armies converged from the West and from the East in the year 1943 to set free North Africa and make open the way for the assault upon Southern Europe.

The site of Medjez el Bab has always been a prize in battles for it overlooks the Medjerda river which is the only one in the whole country which flows all year round. It feeds the fertile Medjerda Valley before it reaches the sea, some 30 miles south of Bizerta. Further south the water courses are merely oueds which often dry up completely in the summer.

Testour, 50 miles from Tunis and also on the Medjerda river, has an Andalusian air for it was settled by the Moors who were driven out from Spain by the Roman Catholic Kings during the fourteenth century. Many of the houses are tiled in Spanish style and a musical 'Festival of Malouf' is held every June in the attractive Café Andalous. The Great Mosque has an unusual minaret of Arab and Spanish design with colourful tilework. A charming sundial tells the hours in one of the two courtyards.

The countryside around Dougga is largely wooded and at Teboursouk a sign points to it some nine kilometres (six miles) away. Then you begin to climb lacets edged with olive groves and fig trees. Finally in the distance high above you can see slender pillars. More and more of them appear as you continue to climb, their honey colour glowing in the sunlight, many joined together by graceful pediments. Dougga rises in tiers on the slopes of a mountain top, a glorious sight, one of the most important cities of Roman Africa to be seen today.

Save for a large car park, a small museum and the custodian's office, which are all next to each other below the theatre, there are no turnstiles, fences or soft drink stands to destroy the scene. There is a very nice café tucked away where it does not obtrude and the attendant will point it out to you. The site faces south about 2,000 feet above sea level and commands some magnificent views. The surrounding landscape slopes gently downward covered in olive and fig groves, scrubby trees and here and there tiny white cube houses, like lumps of sugar. In the valley the oued Khalid edges some marble quarries.

The ruins of this small Roman town, built in the reign of the Emperor Septimus Severus during the second century, cover a site some 800 by 500 metres. Part of the charm is doubtless that trees and shrubs have been allowed to grow where they may. Indeed the theatre and auditorium are edged to one side by two large eucalyptus trees. Wild flowers and tufts of grass grow through the stone crevices and chinks in the walls lessening and softening the ravages of time and neglect.

From the car park it is easiest to go up towards the theatre first. It was built about A.D. 168 and is not large by Roman standards. There is mosaic flooring by the entrance which has been faded to a grey by the sun. It could accommodate 3,500 people in 23 tiers of seats which are divided by three aisles. It still does so for there is a summer festival each year when there are performances of French classics or Greek tragedies. The Comédie Française has appeared several times on its white marble inlaid stage. The French archaeologist I. Poinssot restored the theatre in 1910.

The best preserved building is that of The Capitol with its temple dedicated to Jupiter, Juno and Minerva. Eleven steep steps lead up to it and you enter under an ornate pediment through honey-coloured fluted columns with acanthus leaves capitals. Few photographers can resist taking these against a blue sky.

To the north of the Capitol lie all types of Roman stonework from oil presses to pieces of column which it is hoped one day will be put together with other fragments like a jigsaw puzzle. To the west there are the remains of the Forum edged on three sides by

white marble colonnades. Near this stands the third-century
Severus Alexander arch. Chariot wheel ruts, as so often in Roman
ruins, can be seen but the usual dead straight roads are missing as
these at Dougga were built over Numidian or even Punic founda-
tions and often followed their line.

The Temple of Mercury has three remaining chambers, two
semi-circular and one of rectangular shape. You climb up three
steps to reach its portico. The Temple of Caelestis dates from
A.D. 235 and has been restored in places. It is some 100 metres
from the Forum set in an olive grove.

To the south there are remains of private villas, many with
sections of mosaic flooring, and Roman baths.

The House of the Trefoil is one of the largest dwellings and
believed to have been a brothel. Twenty-one steps lead up to it
and it has chambers around a central court which at one time
must have contained fountains and flower beds. Near this building there are the thermal 'Baths of Cyclops' so named because of
a mosaic uncovered here and now in the Bardo museum. Two
other mosaics discovered at Dougga and now in the Bardo are of
similar myths. One shows Dionysus being attacked by pirates and
the other depicts Ulysses, tied to the mast of his ship to save him
from succumbing to the song of the Sirens, struggling to get free
of his bonds. His sailors, their ears plugged with wax, cannot hear
the sound and are rowing the God out of danger.

Also in the Baths of the Cyclops there is a horseshoe-shaped
public convenience which can seat a dozen people at one time,
which conjures up an odd picture of a dual purpose convention
being held in informal surroundings.

The Berber-Punic Mausoleum is earlier than the Roman
remains and believed to date from the second century B.C. It is
some 70 feet high and has been reconstructed. Its original inscription is in the British Museum and is in Phoenician script.

From Dougga, if you join the Highway G.P. 5 again and follow
it south-west, it carries on to Le Kef (The Cliff) some 25 miles from
the Algerian frontier. This town, with its 20,000 inhabitants,
sprawls down a hillside. In the last World War it was the base

20   *Lighthouse and date palms, Jerba*

from which a provisional Tunisian government held out against Vichy and later it became the headquarters of the Free French.

Thermal springs have been known here since Roman times and those who have visited the underground colonnaded cisterns of Istanbul will find the ones at Le Kef their counterpart, although on a smaller scale. Also they are dry except for occasional rain water. The mosaic linings of the baths are protected with sand. Much excavation work remains to be done and in due course perhaps the blocked source of the springs will be found once more. It is believed to have been near the Mellegue river and reached Le Kef at a temperature of 38° Centigrade.

Little pavement cafés are in evidence and beyond a small park, blue gates lead to one of President Bourguiba's summer residences. Along to the left of this the white domes edged with green tiling of the Sidi Mizouni mosque, which has been turned into a library, come into view.

The fourteenth-century Sidi Bou Makhlouf mosque is one beloved by artists with its faience decorated minaret and twin fluted domes. The minaret is polygonal with a crenellated gallery where the muezzin sings his call to prayer. A slender tower above this has two rims of crenellated edging before culminating in a point. The mosque is reached by a wide flight of steps edged by white buildings with arched doorways and nail decorated doors. Wrought iron lanterns light the way at night.

Back on the highway one passes many Berber villages but they do not have the same romantic appeal as the Bedouin encampments which you see in other regions. The latter appear first as small blobs of black far away on the flat stony waste. On closer inspection they seem to be barren open spaces but in fact are divided into well defined grazing grounds by the Bedouin with special boundaries between the tribes which no European could identify.

Ruth Aldridge, a well-known caravaner and writer, told me of a visit she made to a Bedouin family. She was taken by a Tunisian friend and, some fifty feet away from the tent where they had been invited, he stopped her at a row of stones placed in a semicircle

21   The Severus Alexander arch in the Roman town of Dougga

on the ground. 'This is the "front gate",' he explained, 'and it is polite to wait here until our host walks forward to greet us.'

A tall, white bearded Arab, a dignified figure in a long white robe, came to meet them. Courtesies were exchanged and the Bedouin shook hands and led them towards his tent. There his two daughters-in-law and their five children waited shyly. The young men of the family were away working. A mule, grazing on a crop of prickly pear a short distance away was near another woman who was minding a flock of scrawny sheep and goats. The old man waved his hands in her direction. 'Our only camel was drowned during the last floods,' he explained, 'we shall be able to afford one later if it is God's will.' On either side of the tent entrance brushwood was piled high. An old oil drum, chained to a boulder for anchorage, contained the water supply. This was replenished each day by women from the nearest well three miles away. A small fire had been kindled and the guests were invited to sit around. It was made between three flat stones with appetising smells coming from blackened cooking pots on top. Hand woven bedding was spread out to air on the piles of brushwood. The tent itself stretched into position over rough wooden poles, was woven from sheep's wool in natural colours ranging from pale fawn to dark brown.

When the meal was finished Ruth asked one of the Bedouin women, who spoke a little French, where she kept her most precious possessions. 'Come and see,' was the smiling reply. Ruth followed her into the tent. It was scrupulously clean and bare save for several brightly woven rugs. On top of some orange boxes lay a battered old suitcase. The woman opened it reverently as though it was a casket of jewels. Inside lay some neatly folded silk robes. 'My wedding clothes,' said the woman. Most of the space was taken up by a small stack of well-used books. 'These,' said the woman picking them up gently and holding them to her heart, 'these are my greatest possessions. They are my children's schoolbooks. Every day they walk three miles to the village to school and three miles back. I cannot read or write – but my children will.'

12. The Northern Coast

Bizerta, near the northernmost point of Africa, is in a commanding position in the narrowest part of the Mediterranean. It is 714 miles east of Gibraltar and 240 miles north-west of Malta and is one of the world's finest harbours. When the French captured it in 1881 a statesman, Jules Ferry, remarked, 'This port and this lake are worth the whole of the rest of Tunisia. If I have taken Tunisia, it is to have Bizerta!' Between the two Great World Wars France considered Bizerta to be the most important naval base in the Mediterranean after Toulon.

It is one of Tunisia's oldest cities and saw plenty of wars with Carthage. The Phoenicians first opened up the land-locked Lake of Bizerta, which is about 4½ miles wide and eight miles long with an average depth of 36 feet, and this well protected anchorage reaching the sea was one of the reasons the French found it of such strategic importance.

In the seventh century the port was conquered by the Arabs and from that time was subject to the rulers of Tunis or of Constantinople. The inhabitants were insubordinate and unruly and eventually threw in their lot with the pirate Khair-ed-Din, one of the famous Barbarossa brothers. It is said that on one raid to Malta two hundred Knights were brought back to Bizerta as captives and held in the Kasbah until a high ransom was paid for their return.

Today, surrounded by hills, Bizerta is a mixture of broad tree-lined avenues with fountains on the one hand and narrow streets, stone-built houses and cool courtyards on the other. The Corniche, with sand dunes stretching from the town, has several modern hotels set in delightfully landscaped gardens and a new Congress Hall with committee rooms, large auditorium and theatre. A few miles offshore, lies the island of Cani, an ideal place for underwater fishing.

When the Moors were flung out of Spain during the fifteenth and sixteenth centuries, many of them settled here. The Andalusian quarter still retains its Spanish atmosphere with attractive nail-decorated doors, arched alleyways, wrought iron grille work, and winding streets. To the west lies the Spanish Fort built in 1573 and now converted into a theatre, and to the North the Sidi Salem Fort. The Moors set up their craft centres outside the Medina walls and their descendants, three hundred years later, continue to work in the same place today.

In the maze of the Medina there are the usual colourful things to bargain for, handworked copper and brassware, gay carpets, aromatic spices, sheepskin rugs, long kaftans and leatherware. The picturesque old harbour is the focal point and near it there is a famous black and white marble fountain which has an inscription in Arabic and Turkish extolling the goodness and sweetness of the water and inviting passers-by to sample it.

The Kasbah, built between the thirteenth and seventeenth centuries, overlooks the old port with blank walls facing the quays and its entrance in the Place du Marche. An archway leads into a vaulted passage with bends and turns to repel invaders. The Great Mosque with an octagonal minaret was built during the seventeenth century. In the prayer hall there is a holy black stone against which believers can rub themselves if they are ill instead of performing the usual ritual ablutions.

Much of the residential part of the town is new, having been rebuilt from the devastation of the 1939-45 War. The population is some 47,000 and many of the women are completely veiled. The local carpets are knotted on frames as a cottage industry and arrangements for a visit can be made. There is a handicraft centre in the Rue d'Algerie. Embroidery, sandals and slippers are good buys. Modern shops line the Avenue Habib Bourguiba and are open 9 a.m. to noon and 3 p.m. to 9 p.m. Facing the same avenue is the central synagogue, the convent block of the Institution Saint Marie and Martyrs' Square.

For entertainment there is dancing every Saturday night at the Club Sport Nautique, nightly at the Hotel Corniche, and at the discotheque Petit Mousse and you can find several outside cafés and little café bars. The Muncipal stadium has occasional football matches and sporting events.

Bizerta is an easy town in which to drive. It is simple to maintain one's sense of direction by reference to the coast and the inland lake. The channel connecting the latter to the outer harbour and the sea is crossed by two efficient drive-on, drive-off ferries for which no charge is made. The crossing takes only four minutes, loading and unloading is swift and trouble free and one of the ferries maintains a service all night.

A pleasant scenic round drive from Bizerta which covers some ten miles is along the coast road to Cape Bizerta, Cape Blanc and back through Nador. The views are lovely and you pass the grottoes where the townspeople often sought shelter during 1941 and 1942. At one time during the war Bizerta suffered 250 air raids in 173 days. As a short diversion there is the radio communication station on the top of Jebel Nador which is some 860 feet high and can be reached up a twisty rough road.

Another drive is around Lake Bizerta to Lake Ichkeul then through Tindja and Menzel Bourguiba a distance of about 36 miles. Bizerta is connected by a long channel to an area of blackish water, Garaat el Ichkeul, which is shallow in places with many little reed islets. These attract water fowl of different kinds. Across the water the wooded Jebel Ichkeul rises to 2,000 feet. Legend has it that this mountain, desiring to be alone, left its fellows and settled by the water.

Jebel Ichkeul was a royal hunting reserve since the thirteenth century. In 1729 a pair of buffaloes was sent to the Bey as a gift from the King of Sicily. The Bey set them free on the mountain. There they thrived and multiplied but were decimated by General

Bradley's troops in 1942. However, several survived and a new herd has grown up since then.

From Bizerta you can visit Utica 20 miles away or indeed go there from Tunis as the mileage is about the same. Utica was a Phoenician colony founded about 1100 B.C. by Tyre some three centuries before Carthage. When later Queen Dido left Tyre she and her entourage, including a hundred virgins from Cyprus to help people her new domain, bypassed Utica and founded Carthage nearby. The two colonies were great rivals. Utica sided with Caesar during the first Punic War but remained neutral during the third and so avoided the destruction that overcame Carthage, the Romans subsequently making it their capital in North Africa. In A.D. 46 the younger Cato, allied to the Numidians, remained in Utica during the final struggle against Caesar and, when the Numidians scattered, he committed suicide.

The name 'Utica' means the 'Ancient' or the 'Magnificent'. Of coins unearthed a number have had Punic legends and heads of Castor and Pollux on them. Later ones have Latin legends and the heads of Livia and Tiberius. The city was the seat of a bishop and had its Christian martyrs from the third century onwards. Silt brought down by the Medjerda river gradually converted Utica's splendid harbour into a shallow anchorage and the process has gone so far over the years that today Utica is over eight miles inland.

As Rome declined so the town lost its importance and, with the coming of the Vandals, the Byzantines and then the Arab invasion in A.D. 698, the town was practically depopulated. After the eighth century those who remained succumbed to fever.

Today the ruins covering a small plateau are all that remain of Utica. Yet it is a charming place to visit, especially at sunset. Shattered beauty is all that is left of the ancient magnificence, but the scattered ruins, broken masonry, prostrate pillars and fallen capitols cannot but stir the emotions. Thomas Whateley wrote as long ago as 1770 'A monument of antiquity, is never seen with indifference. . . .'

One of the reasons that Utica is so touching is because there are no railed enclosures, no turnstiles or kiosks, no youths pestering you to buy fake relics and no persistent guides. An aged gardener-custodian lifted wooden shutters off the ground for me to see the mosaics beneath. These once formed the bottoms of pools, basins and fountains, usually with charming fish designs. The custodian wetted his forefinger with his tongue and rubbed it gently over a fish to enhance its brilliant colour. He pointed out to me where the sun has faded some of the exposed mosaics. The outstanding features are the arch of the gateway, several sturdy columns, por-ticos, broken walls and sections of paved streets. Geraniums inter-mingle with fragments of pillars. Wild flowers and grasses grow up between blocks of stone. One section of ground had three different pieces of mosaic flooring, each of a different period and dug at different levels. Two of the well-preserved mosaic murals have been removed to the Bardo museum. One is of Diana the goddess of hunting and wild life who, it is said, ranged her beloved forests attended by her nymphs. The mosaic shows her about to loose an arrow on an innocent deer who is nibbling leaves off a tree. The reader may remember that she was almost as famous for her chastity as her hunting. According to fable Actaeon, while out hunting with his hounds, came upon her bathing in the nude. She was so outraged that, forgetting for the moment what she stood for, she changed him into a stag whereupon he was torn to pieces by his own hounds.

The other mosaic, which is third-century, depicts Neptune and his queen in their marine chariots. The top of the picture shows him raising his kingly head above the waves with a worried expres-sion while two cherubs fly from his shoulders and ride off joyously on dolphins.

To revert to Utica, near the entrance of the site are the founda-tions of a palatial mansion known as the 'House of the Waterfall'. The inner courtyard had a fountain from which water flowed over a sloping mosaic surface decorated with plump, lively fish. The fish motif occurs again and again in Tunisian mosaics and the designs are invariably delightful. It may be thought that too much emphasis has been put on mosaics in describing Tunisian ruins but they are an especial feature of the Roman period here when the art reached heights not known before. Also, because of the great wealth of colours in North African marbles, artistic talent was given free rein and some of the world's finest mosaic work has been found during excavations in Carthage and Utica. Reds are of four different shades and there are an equal number of yellows and greens, the last colour in all its tints being exclusive to this part of the globe. The colours of some of the mosaic work are quiet and harmonious with gradations of tints suggesting light and shade with artistic skill. Deep blacks, browns and bluish greys are also used. The designs are as full of innovation as the shading is subtle with large spaces filled with acanthus and other leaves in sweeping curves.

The Utica site is most uneven to walk around and, surprisingly, the necropolis suddenly drops some 15 feet below the rest of the ruins. Steps lead down to several Punic sandstone tombs, some nine feet long and covered with stone slabs. One still contains a skeleton with some domestic objects.

It is difficult to decide if it is better to visit the antiquarium and the lapidary museum before going over the site or afterwards. The former has a modest collection of pottery, statuettes, coins and other objects arranged according to period. Some mosaic murals are shown in situ.

En route back to Bizerta after seeing Utica you can make another excursion off to the right of G.P. 8 to visit Raf Raf and Ghar el Melh – also known as Porto Farina. The latter was a Phoenician settlement and suburb of Utica. Natural saltpans give the town its name which means 'salt grotto'. During the seventeenth century corsairs sought shelter on the nearby lake between raiding parties. This has now silted up. Three Turkish strongholds still remain which acted as prisons for pirates' captives while awaiting ransom or being sold as slaves. These were heavily bombarded in 1655 when Admiral Blake sought to release English prisoners. Beyond the fishing port the road narrows and follows a palm-fringed shore line likened to Polynesia by many visitors. Certainly it is exotic for the white sandy beach stretches as far as the

22   *The Capitol, Dougga*

eye can see and the little town itself is picturesque with its arch-ways, fountains and seventeenth-century mosque.

Raf Raf, clearly signposted, is a hilltop town overlooking the sea. The women are known for their fine lacework and the making of couscous cooking pots of terracotta. They wear local robes of red and purple. Vineyards sweep along the lower slopes of the hillside to the sea and produce a grape which makes a very fine white wine. Here as always there is a good beach for swimming and under-water pursuits. About a mile or so offshore the uninhabited island of Pilau has vertical sides like an iceberg.

From Bizerta to Tabarka, near the Algerian border. can be a one-day jaunt of about 90 miles along the highways G.P. 11, M.C. 51, M.C. 66 and finally G.P. 7. It is about 110 miles from Tunis and its old castle ruins recall its mixed history of being occupied in turn by the Phoenicians, the Genoese, the Turks and the Arabs. Coral fishing is traditional in this little port encircled by mountains and the sea. Needless to say with such a background it was the haunt of pirates. It acted as a base for Allied forces from Algeria in 1942 and 1943 but today is a peaceful place for holidays with splendid beaches, good bathing, fishing and hunting in the wild forests which coat its surrounding mountains.

There is an annual summer festival during July and August for holiday makers at a hut village along the shore in a pine wood which can accommodate up to 2,500 people. There is horse-riding, sailing and other water and underwater pursuits. No car traffic is allowed within the village where there is an Andalusian coffee bar, theatre on the green, open-air cinema, basilica, circus and other types of entertainment. Workshops are a new innovation where holiday makers can try their hand at sculpture, painting, Tunisian cooking, dramatic art or photography. International artists pro-vide entertainment and a full programme is worked out for eight weeks that tries to suit all tastes.

The forests of Khroumiria are famous for their cork trees and you can watch it being loaded at the port. The Hotel de France is well known for its atmosphere created by its former owner a

23   'Ghorfas'
24   Bizerta harbour

famous French hunter named Abatte, who decorated the dining-room walls like a hunting lodge with stuffed heads of wild-boar and smaller game. Here also President Bourguiba with two colleagues, Hedi Chaker and Mongi Slim, were placed under house arrest in 1952. Their favourite table is pointed out to you.

A hunting party for wild boar sounds like the old days of pig sticking in India or, even further back, Merrie England, when the ancient forest laws under the Norman kings made the poaching of wild boar punishable by death or the loss of a limb. Even today the boar's head is considered a special delicacy and its serving is attended with much ceremony. For many centuries, owing to its great strength, speed and ferocity, the wild boar has been one of the favourite beasts of the chase. Today you can hunt it on the outskirts of Tabarka at Ain Draham with beaters waving flags and letting off fire crackers. There are drives in the morning, a stop for lunch and then perhaps two drives in the afternoon. One English party last season ended the day with a boar and sow weighing 130 pounds each. Enquiries should be made at the Tunisian Tourist Office in the country of departure before leaving on holiday about the import of firearms, ammunition and the issue of permits. For animal watchers and photographers there are deer, lynx and wild cat in the area.

The lakes between Bizerta and Tabarka are a refuge for wildfowl which rest here on their annual migrations. Not only the sportsman but the ornithologist and naturalist will find the lakes entrancing for they harbour teal, shoveller, goose, golden plover and many other water fowl. Snipe swoop down over the wheat-fields as well as woodcock, partridge and turtle doves.

For those who are unable to visit Tabarka the first time they go to Tunisia nothing is more evocative of the port than a lovely mosaic in the Bardo museum called 'Country House'. It is fan-shaped edged with green leaves. It shows a type of castle-cum-mansion with twin turrets joined by an arcaded gallery. This is surrounded by a green luxuriant forest which harbours mythical and real wildfowl.

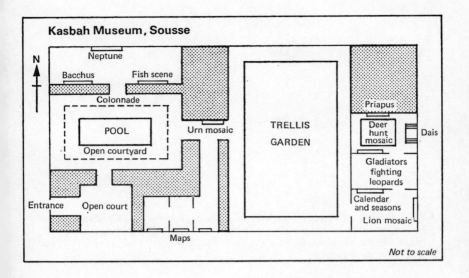

Kasbah Museum, Sousse

N

Neptune
Bacchus
Fish scene
Colonnade
POOL
Open courtyard
Urn mosaic
TRELLIS GARDEN
Priapus
Deer hunt mosaic
Dais
Gladiators fighting leopards
Calendar and seasons
Lion mosaic
Entrance
Open court
Maps

Not to scale

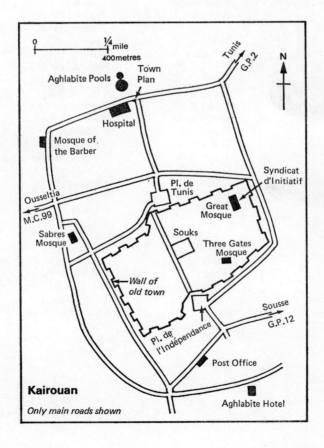

0 ¼ mile
400 metres

Aghlabite Pools
Town Plan
Hospital
Mosque of the Barber
Ousseltia
M.C.99
Sabres Mosque
Pl. de Tunis
Souks
Great Mosque
Three Gates Mosque
Syndicat d'Initiatif
Wall of old town
Pl. de l'Indépendance
Post Office
Aghlabite Hotel
Tunis
G.P.2
N
Sousse
G.P.12

Kairouan

Only main roads shown

Glossary

The spelling of Arabic words is of course phonetic in English and is bound to cause many pitfalls. It is inevitable that different spellings will occur for the same name or place in maps, this book and signposts. The following may help.

Phonetic Spelling	Pronunciation	Meaning
Aid	A-ee-d	Feast
Alfalfon		Esparto grass
Bab	Bab	Door
Bahira	Barheera	Sea
Ben		Son of (see Ibn)
Bir	Beer	Well
Bled		Countryside
Bordj	Borge	Fort or castle
Chechia	Sheshia	Red skull cap
Chott	Shot	Salt lake
Choukran	Shookrarn	Thank you
Dar		Large house or palace
Dir	Deer	Table land
Djamas	Jarmarse	Mosque
Djemell	Jemel	Camel
Enfida	Enfeeder	Ravine
Fandook		Inn
Fernana	Fairnarnar	Cork oak forest
Ghar	Gar	Cave
Ghorfa	Gorfa	Arched cave dwelling
Hadj	Hadge	Pilgrim to Mecca
Hamma	Hammer	Hot spring
Hammam		Turkish bath
Ibn	Iben	Son of (see Ben)
Jebel		Hill
Jerid	Jerrid	Countryside with palm trees
Kebir	Kebeer	Large

Kef	Keff	Cliff
La	Lar	No
Lalla	Lalla	Female saint
Ma	Mar	Water
Mabrouk	Marbrook	Congratulations
Madrasah	Mardrarsar	Mosque and school combined
Malouf	Marloof	Andalusian music
Medina	Medeena	Arab town
Medjez	Medjez	Ferry or ford
Menzel		Jerban beehive house
Mezwed		Bagpipes
Mihrab	Meerarb	Niche in a mosque
Minbar		Pulpit in mosque
Mudhala	Moodarlar	Type of straw hat
Muezzin	Mwezeen	Priest who calls the faithful to prayer
Oued	Wed	River
Rabat		Fortified monastery
Rabba		Market square
Ras	Ras	Headland
Riadh	Reeyard	Garden
Sabra	Sarbrar	Desert
Sahel	Sarhell	Seashore
Said	Sayead	Happy
Salaam	Salarm	Greeting
Sidi	Seedee	Lord or noble
Skhoun	Skoon	Hot
Souk	Sook	Market
Soumaa	Soomar	Minaret
Sour	Soor	Ramparts
Tell		Hill
Yemeen		Right
Yssar	Issar	Left
Zawia	Zaweear	Shrine
Zitoun	Zitoon	Olive

Index